SILVER HAIR & GOLDEN VOICE

AUSTIN WILLIS

From Halifax to Hollywood

As *told to* ERNEST J. DICK

Foreword by COSTAS HALAVREZOS
Afterword By RON FOLEY MACDONALD

NIMBUS
PUBLISHING
— NIMBUS.CA —

Nimbus Publishing Limited
3660 Strawberry Hill Street, Halifax, NS, B3K 5A9
(902) 455-4286 nimbus.ca

Printed and bound in Canada
NB1468
Cover and interior design: John van der Woude Designs
Editor: Angela Mombourquette

Library and Archives Canada Cataloguing in Publication

Title: Silver hair and golden voice : Austin Willis, from Halifax to Hollywood / as told to Ernest J. Dick ; foreword by Costas Halavrezos.
Names: Dick, Ernest J., author.
Identifiers: Canadiana (print) 20200161970
Canadiana (ebook) 20200161997 | ISBN 9781771088527 (softcover)
ISBN 9781771088534 (HTML)
Subjects: LCSH: Willis, Austin. | LCSH: Motion picture actors and actresses—Canada—Biography. | LCGFT: Biographies.
Classification: LCC PN2308.W55 D53 2020 | DDC 791.4302/8092—dc23

Canada Council   Conseil des arts
for the Arts   du Canada

Nimbus Publishing acknowledges the financial support for its publishing activities from the Government of Canada, the Canada Council for the Arts, and from the Province of Nova Scotia. We are pleased to work in partnership with the Province of Nova Scotia to develop and promote our creative industries for the benefit of all Nova Scotians.

*All photos courtesy the Austin Willis Collection,
Saint Mary's University Archives, Halifax*

Contents

Foreword

by COSTAS HALAVREZOS

Most often, a foreword is written by a friend or colleague *after* reading the author's manuscript. However, I'm tapping this out before the book's even been written, as both a challenge and an act of faith.

And because I miss Austin Willis.

In 1999, I received a call from my friend Blackford Parker. He asked, "Do you know the name 'Austin Willis'?" Of course, I did, as most people of my generation—and even those much older—would. Over a long career in Canada and internationally, Austin's performances on radio, stage, television, and film had earned the attention of successive audiences, from Halifax to Hollywood. Blackford continued: "Do you know that he's retired and living in Dartmouth?" I didn't and was momentarily stunned. Imagine—a giant of Canadian performing arts, mere blocks away from my home! And since I was still working as a broadcaster with CBC Radio, my next thought leapt to the possibility of interviewing him. Blackford had anticipated this and had a phone number at the ready.

But rather than cold-call Austin Willis, I first got on the phone to Ern Dick, the CBC's former (and only) Corporate Archivist. He had allegedly retired to Granville Ferry, Nova Scotia, but was always researching and executing myriad projects—everything from a radio series, the *History of Sound,* and an oral history of *Singalong Jubilee* to a university course on Atlantic Canadian Film and a multimedia installation for a rural museum. The news of Austin's proximity was greeted with Ern's signature restraint: "Austin Willis! In Dartmouth? Wow!!"

When I eventually called Austin's number, it was disconcerting, but also magical, to hear that distinctive baritone on the line. I introduced myself, and he greeted this stranger like an old friend—a cordiality that calmed nervousness. I asked if he might allow Ern and me to interview him about his career, and he graciously agreed. He and his wife, Gwen, welcomed us for several sessions of recording and note-taking at their home, accompanied by tea and cookies. But those treats were often left neglected because we were so enchanted by Austin's stories.

Ern and I each had our personal reference points for Austin's career: the frequent lead in CBC-TV's ambitious dramas throughout the 1950s and '60s (because of his prematurely white hair, Austin was often cast "older" than he was); the first host of *Cross-Canada Hit Parade;* the man who bested Goldfinger at cards (with help from Sean Connery's James Bond); the debonair, wry host of the TV quiz show *This Is The Law* in the '70s.

During the interviews, Austin had a deft way of turning the spotlight away from himself while relating fascinating anecdotes involving luminaries he'd worked with—from Orson Welles and Peter Sellers to a young William Shatner (his subordinate in *Space Command*—CBC's precursor to *Star Trek*). There was never a whiff of name-dropping, nor a remark designed to taint a colleague's reputation. When he told us about his time as a radio announcer in the early days of the Second World War (before he served in the navy), it was about a terrible on-air mistake he made—reading the right commercial, but in an unfortunate context, considering the newscast about a sunken allied ship which preceded it (a pertinent argument for making TV newscasts ad-free zones).

Austin almost compulsively sidestepped every opportunity to burnish his reputation. When he had the lead in a hit play in London's West End, he chose to tell us about the show when he "dried" (forgot his lines)—one of the perils for actors in long-running productions. A Western shot in Mexico allowed him to point out how inept he was whenever he was required to saddle up and ride off for the cameras; but then we were spellbound as he described an intriguing behind-the-scenes cast which featured (a) McCarthy-era blacklisted scriptwriters using assumed names, (b) a one-man security detail provided by John Wayne, and (c) his boyhood idol Roy Rogers, who made a dramatic pre-dawn appearance to personally deliver a docile horse from the herd he maintained to service the movie industry in Mexico.

But this wealth of historical intelligence and the masterful way Austin related it had a peculiar effect on Ern and me. We always came away feeling like characters in the parable of the five blind men describing an elephant. Each new revelation underlined the fact that we had entered this project with only the merest understanding of the extent to which Austin had been a witness to, and participant in, the twentieth century's revolutionary changes in the performing arts and media.

So here's the challenge to the author: if people like us—who had seen and heard Austin perform in his heyday—had so little appreciation of the breadth and depth of his career, why would someone who wasn't familiar with him have the slightest inclination to read your book about someone born a few months before the Halifax Explosion? (And yes, there's a story about that, too.)

We live in an era of "peak celebrity." There is no theatrical craft involved in becoming, for example, a Bachelor or Bachelorette, who traipses through the unreality of a "reality" TV series and, win or lose, becomes a household name. Who will spare the time to learn about a person who isn't around to greet us from magazine covers in the checkout line or to clog our Instagram and Twitter feeds with selfies?

But I'm filled with faith that Austin's marvellous stories will receive a new, well-deserved audience because they're in the hands of Ern Dick and the formidable arts and culture commentator Ron Foley Macdonald. For more than thirty years, Ron has been writing, critiquing, and curating, as well as teaching, stage and film. He's shared his talents with the Atlantic Film Festival, the Canada Council, the CBC, and the NFB, and has contributed to Halifax newspapers and the *Globe and Mail*. Ron's interests were enriched by Austin Willis's insights and insider information on the performing arts and on the people he'd worked with in radio, stage, movies, and TV.

The foreword often seems to act as a speed bump, impeding your desire to get to cruising speed with the book that lies ahead. But in this case, I hope this foreword serves as an invitation to journey through the landscape of the past century's huge transformations in entertainment and media, as witnessed by the most charming and experienced guide you could imagine— Austin Willis.

Austin Willis Comes to Granville Ferry

by ERNEST J. DICK

Austin Willis arrived in Granville Ferry, Nova Scotia, in September 1999 looking splendid—fresh off a 1950s-era Hollywood film set, or so it seemed. He was wearing the camel hair coat that he loved so much. There was not a strand of his iconic wavy white hair out of place, nor a wrinkle on his eighty-two-year-old face, which featured a bigger, more confident, more permanent smile than we had ever seen in rural Nova Scotia.

I was more than a little apprehensive! I had convinced the folks at King's Theatre in Annapolis Royal (across the Annapolis Basin from Granville Ferry) to host an evening in which Austin Willis would share memories of his life.

Before I'd received Costas's call telling me Austin Willis was living in Dartmouth, I had been promoting, researching, preserving, and presenting the legacy of Canadian broadcasting and film for more than forty years but only vaguely remembered the name Austin Willis—and nothing in my formidable library had told me much more. My records had lots to say about "Brother" J. Frank Willis, but it seemed to me Austin had slipped into a well-deserved obscurity.

Nonetheless, as a conscientious archivist and an oral historian, it had been irresistible to talk with Austin in Halifax. In the years leading up to this performance, I had interviewed Austin Willis about his decades of experience many times and had been quickly and completely enchanted by his stories—but then I am easily charmed by any stories of broadcasting, film, or performance. Austin had a poignant and authentic experience related to every person and any title or program I could think to ask him about—and I was full of questions, recording every word.

Austin Willis had retired to Dartmouth, across the harbour from his birthplace in Halifax, after having lived in Toronto, London (England), the Westwood area of Los Angeles, and Wetaskiwin, Alberta. He had been active on stage, on radio, on television, and on film; I eventually compiled a timeline of more than two hundred entries for his six decades of performing (you can read a slightly condensed version of this timeline on page 135).

Preparing for his one-man show would prove challenging. Austin had rarely seen or heard himself—having done much of his performing before the days of video recording and well before the proliferation of media through digitization. Indeed, Austin had been so busy that he had only a precious few playbills and publicity shots from his career. Certainly he had no correspondence, scripts, fan letters, or reviews that could help inform his recollections for the upcoming King's Theatre performance. But as a moving image and sound archivist, I knew whom to ask—and found for him many examples of his work, which helped Austin recall specific periods in his long and varied career. These are now organized and available for research at the Saint Mary's University Archives—and Austin Willis was so pleased to know that.

But would audiences see Austin Willis as a sad and unfortunate relic of an earlier time? We live in an era of hyper-current information—and indulging bygone days in broadcasting and performance is not a priority for many of us. Also, Austin Willis played pomp and pretense so convincingly that few might be willing to be charmed by him. Maybe Austin Willis deserved a rest—or perhaps he needed to be forgotten?

And who would Austin Willis become on the stage of King's Theatre? Many an actor is petrified of being himself on stage, and Austin Willis had good reason. He had always played the supporting role, whether to his celebrity panel on *This Is The Law,* or to Peter Sellers, Charles Boyer, Orson Welles, and dozens of others. Could he even go on stage by himself?

I knew that Austin had spellbinding stories of all of this, but would his reflexive self-deprecation hold anyone's interest? Austin Willis openly admitted that he had chain-smoked too many Matinée cigarettes (the sponsor of his long-time radio program) and drunk too much strong drink in his earlier days. Who was he now—now that he was living in Nova Scotia after being away for sixty years?

His wife, Gwen, had come to Granville Ferry with him—doing the driving and much else that Austin needed. Austin was so charming and engaging that he had almost always been married— and almost always been working. He'd had royalties coming in regularly over the years but had no "hits" to keep him and his wives living in grand style. Any property Austin had purchased eventually became his modest legacy for his spouses. Not that he would speak to me of any of this—though I did always wonder how and why these marriages never seemed to last. He was candid and loving about how his marriage to Kate Reid became a casualty of the stresses that afflict a two-career family in the acting business—and I didn't need to know the details.

Austin Willis loved a good cigarette.

In leading the way to Hollywood, Austin Willis was a mentor to Gordon Pinsent, Jimmy Doohan ("Scotty" of *Star Trek* fame), William Shatner, and undoubtedly many other Canadian actors.

I invited anyone I could contact to remember Austin—but all had forgotten Austin Willis in their own successes. Maybe it was kinder to allow Austin Willis to remain forgotten?

I knew Austin Willis would charm my wife, Nancy, and our friends when he came to dinner before the performance, and he did. He was the perfect dinner guest. Austin loved food, particularly strong cheeses—but he could also be distracted by questions about anyone we might ask about. It became almost a game to see who might stump Austin—but he had stories of everyone from Elvis Presley to Beatrice Lillie, and of many performers whose names none of us recognized (though I eventually researched them). Only Bing Crosby caused him to stop. Yes, he knew Bing Crosby well—but would say nothing beyond that. Austin fundamentally believed that if he couldn't say something gracious or kind about a person, he would say nothing at all—an old-school quality that is decidedly out of fashion in our trash-talking twenty-first century.

Our evenings onstage were not going to divulge any secrets! Not provoke any headlines!

Who would Austin Willis now be?

Well, when he stepped into the spotlight at King's Theatre, Austin Willis was Austin Willis—a man who'd lived through the evolution of the stages, airwaves, and screens of the twentieth century. No one had ever asked him to tell his own life story—and the first telling is invariably the freshest and most thoughtful. He was funny and regretful, thoughtful and ironic, self-deprecating, and never triumphant or self-important. Austin was as eager to please as he had been for all of his audiences and his fellow performers—and with an authenticity that left us all feeling like we were his friends.

Nobody knew that the well-crafted, emotional performance they'd just witnessed had been unrehearsed. Well-prepared, yes, but unrehearsed.

Austin Willis finally had his triumph on stage "being Austin Willis"—though Austin would never have used such pretentious phrasing.

It was my proudest and happiest moment as chair of King's Theatre.

The preeminent historian of Atlantic Canada, Colin Howell, also came to believe in Austin Willis. Colin was the executive director of the Gorsebrook Research Institute for Atlantic Canadian Studies (now the Gorsebrook Research Institute) at Saint Mary's University (smu). With his involvement, we reprised "An Evening with Austin Willis" at Saint Mary's as a fundraiser for the Gorsebrook Institute. A few of Austin's surviving posters have since adorned the Austin Willis Meeting Room at smu. Colin also secured the resources to produce a short documentary about the life of Austin Willis, which is available for download through the smu Archives. (You can find that thirteen-minute documentary by going to https://tinyurl.com/tmqffpa.)

In 2002, Austin Willis received an honorary doctorate from smu; in that same year he also received Queen Elizabeth ii's Golden Jubilee Medal and the Order of Canada. Austin Willis was finally recognized and appreciated for being Austin Willis back home in Halifax—and in Canada.

In April 2004, when he was in palliative care in Dartmouth, I came to town and called Gwen just to see how Austin was doing. She relayed my greetings to him, and Austin insisted on seeing me. It was during one of those "shut-downs" where hospitals only allow the closest of family to visit—and I was gowned and capped before I could come in. I was determined not to challenge Austin further and instead brought him a story I had found about him in Max Ferguson's 1968 Stephen Leacock Award–winning memoir of broadcasting mishaps, *And Now...Here's Max*. It was a perfectly innocent story, which involved Austin on a slushy Toronto street trying to return a rubber shoe protector to its owner—a man who'd just given him a drive during a transit strike. Austin knew the story but corrected it. It had actually happened to his brother Frank, not him. No one at the CBC could imagine it occurring to J. Frank Willis, the icon of Canadian broadcasting, so it had been attributed to Austin, who was always the butt of all misadventures.

Austin Willis was definitely looking more splendid that weekend in his hospital bed than we were in our hospital gowns. His pyjamas were clean and pressed, and his hair was still in place—and his smile was as big and genuine as ever.

Austin died later that weekend.

That began my campaign to produce a full-scale documentary—but no one was interested. It appeared that Austin Willis was to be forgotten in our virtual, networking, instantaneous twenty-first century. Graciousness, humility, and poignancy are not in vogue these days, and my belief in Austin Willis's story faltered.

But Costas Halavrezos and Ron Foley Macdonald believed in Austin Willis—perhaps even more than I did. This book would not have happened without them, though do not blame them for the Austin Willis that emerges from these pages. Turning my interviews and his one-man show into a legacy invites its own hazards—and I freely admit to the liberties I have taken in transcribing, organizing, and even in putting words into Austin Willis's mouth by telling his story from his point of view. I have had both success and failure in publishing oral history—and the reader here will decide which this is. Certainly I look forward to learning further Austin Willis stories—I appreciate how dynamic history is, whether we are open to it or not. Hopefully we will find a way to make use of digital communications to allow Austin Willis's story to evolve.

In organizing Austin Willis's story I have realized the dozens of further questions I could have, and maybe should have, asked him. I could have been more persistent about dozens of notables beyond Bing Crosby, of whom Austin Willis had further experience but chose not to speak. But that book would be *Austin Willis Revealed* and would not be true to the friend he became.

Rather, this book hopefully positions Austin Willis as the witness he was to the stages, airwaves, and screens of the twentieth century—a witness as gracious and poignant and humble as the man we knew—in the words he spoke himself.

A Word from Austin Willis

I am standing backstage wondering how on earth I might meet the wonderful man who has just been introduced. Thank you, and indeed, I am very pleased to be here. Of course, at my age I am absolutely delighted to be anywhere.

Thank you, Costas, for finding me. Thank you, Ern, for each and every one of your questions—and for your patience. Thank you, Ron, for providing context, which I have often forgotten. And thank you most of all to Gwen, for bringing me home.

I am so pleased to be back onstage.

Isn't this reserved for opera singers?

Audiences attending An Evening with Austin Willis *at King's Theatre in Annapolis Royal and at Convocation Hall at Saint Mary's University in Halifax laughed, cried, cheered, and stood applauding forever.*

ONE

Growing Up in Halifax With "Brother Frank"

My life began dramatically and fortuitously—and it continued in that way.

I was born at the Victoria General Hospital in Halifax on September 30, 1917. One morning a few months later, I was in my cradle in the bow window of my mother's upstairs sitting room in our house at the intersection of Queen and South Streets.

Then, the Halifax Explosion happened.

The window blew in and the shattered glass made little cuts all over my face. This disturbed everyone terribly. The event was emblematic of the rest of my life: things would fall in on me and I, luckily, would survive.

> *At 9:04 A.M. on December 6, 1917, SS Imo collided with the munitions supply ship Mont Blanc in Halifax Harbour, killing two thousand people and leaving nine thousand injured, making it the largest man-made explosion prior to the use of atomic weapons.*

My older brother, Frank, apparently reported to Mother: "The baby has cut himself"—perhaps anticipating his future as a cool and objective reporter. [□]

J. Frank Willis was eight years old when the Halifax Explosion occurred; later, in the 1940s and 1950s, he would go on to become Canada's most iconic and trusted broadcaster, famous for his coverage of Nova Scotia's 1936 Moose River mine disaster. CBS television's legendary Walter Cronkite would adopt a manner, voice, and moustache that were clearly inspired by J. Frank Willis.

Everyone thought Halifax was under attack, and my mother apparently carried me out into the yard for fear that further blasts would be coming. Being in the piano business, we were more fortunate after the blast than most people: my dad and my uncle were able to use the backs and boards from the piano boxes to cover up our windows.

We were lucky to have those piano boards, because a blizzard arrived the next day, compounding the tragedy for Halifax. [□]

The story Brother Frank (as I called him) told for years was that he had been on the way to school that morning and was looking into Mrs. Doody's candy store at the corner of Bland Street and Victoria Road. He may have had a penny to spend and was painstakingly making his selection when the shock of the blast was transmitted through the rock. This window went in on Mrs. Doody, cutting her to pieces, rather than blowing onto Brother Frank.

Piano manufacturer Willis & Co. had been founded in Montreal in 1884 and was making close to three thousand pianos a year by the early 1900s. The Halifax side of the family sold and distributed pianos in the Maritimes and New England.

The Bite of the Acting Bug

Both Frank and I attended King's-Edgehill School in Windsor, NS, and that is where I heard about David Manners. The reverence that the other students had for Manners made a great impression on me.▣ I probably saw him perform first in a film at the grand Capitol Theatre at the foot of Spring Garden Road in Halifax, and his performance convinced me to become an actor. Just the idea of being like David Manners drove me.

> David Manners had been born in Halifax in 1900 and by the 1930s he had become a leading Hollywood star, with roles in Dracula, *opposite Bela Lugosi, and* The Mummy, *with Boris Karloff.*

My brother, though, could never understand why I wanted to act. I idolized Frank in everything. I had *such* a case of hero worship toward him when I was a child— and probably still do. Brother Frank was already a very successful actor in Halifax in those days—but for him, it was just for fun. He always warned me about the pitfalls ahead for anyone trying to make a career on the stage. But David Manners was always in the back of my mind. (I met Manners once in a London restaurant during the war. But like many fans when confronted with someone they idolize, I was so startled I nearly jumped out of my skin. I had nothing to say.) Because I wanted to be an actor, I was involved with anything the Theatre Arts Guild did at the old Garrick Theatre in Halifax.▣ Brother Frank was the

Austin Willis had charisma, even at an early age. This photo was taken circa 1922 or '23.

> Halifax's Theatre Arts Guild is the country's oldest community theatre company.

lead in everything, so I bugged him continuously. I particularly remember playing Lorenzo in a production of *As You Like It* because of the magnificent costume I got to wear! We had many Brits coming over in these days, most often connected with the navy, and they all seemed to have a theatrical bent. It was a most wonderful time to be young and to have your sights on acting.

As You Like It, *Theatre Arts Guild, Halifax, circa 1930s.*

My One-Night Wrestling Career

In the mid-1930s, when I was eighteen, I was spending much of the summer with my brother and his wife at Hubbards Cove, NS. One of the cottages nearest us was occupied by a handsome, beautifully built blond man—John "Dropkick" Murphy, the American wrestler. The Halifax Forum was having a great season of wrestling that year, and Murphy had a routine in which he played the "good guy" and a series of villains would come and fight him. The audience dearly loved to see him beat them.

I was fascinated by this, of course, because it was as much theatre as it was sport, so I set out to get to know Murphy. We became great friends, and he taught me how to wrestle. There was a very hard, flat, solid bit of sand near the cottages and he brought down a big rubber blanket and we worked out on that. His specialty was, as you might suspect, the drop kick. He would jump in the air, kick you with both feet, and then land back on the ring floor. When you were working with him, you would wait

American wrestler John "Dropkick" Murphy, circa 1935.

until the feet were as close as possible, and then fall before the feet hit you. He used to "drop kick" me, and I got so that I could do it very well.

Naturally, we went in to Halifax to see him fight every week. Murphy also began fighting in smaller places around Nova Scotia. Once in Berwick in the Annapolis Valley, his villain, "The Masked Marvel," couldn't appear. He convinced me to become his opponent, and they put a mask on me. The kids in the audience hated "The Masked Marvel"!

I had a pretty good build in those days, but not with all the muscle professional wrestlers have now. Murphy wasn't very muscular, either; he was downright slim. Most of the match was

John "Dropkick" Murphy performing his signature move.

just a lot of nonsense; a lot of shouting and yelling. It was supposed to be a quick bout, and he was going to flatten me with the drop kick we had perfected on the beach at Hubbards.

We started, and everything was coming along fine. One trick he had taught me was to jump up on the ropes and flip over him when he came at me. I would land on my feet and turn around quickly. I did that, but this was a badly made ring, and my foot went right through the floorboard! Murphy didn't know this and decided he was going to drop kick me right then. I couldn't get out of the way. He hit with me both feet, luckily just on the chest—but I went down like I was clobbered. That was the beginning and end of my wrestling career, but it was great fun while it lasted.

Dancer or Target?

My first experience performing professionally onstage beyond Halifax was at Old Orchard Beach, near Portland, Maine. Paula Montoya was a dancer with a band and floor show at the Nova Scotian Hotel. You may not have heard of her, but I remember her well. She was a beautiful Spanish woman, and her dancing partner in the act was her husband, until they broke up and he left in a great huff.

Surprisingly, she asked me a couple of times if I would dance with her. I did, one night, at the Nova Scotian. I didn't think I was very good at all, but she thought I was fine. Paula then invited me to join her for an engagement down at Old Orchard Beach, the popular seaside destination for New Englanders and for families from New Brunswick and Quebec. When my family heard about this, there was quite the uproar—they thought I had run off with a Spanish dancer!

It was an exciting prospect for a young man—four days in the vacation playground, with its touches of New York's Coney

Island. But Paula was—to put it mildly—very quick-tempered. It wasn't long before we had an altercation. She threw a knife at me, actually, and it stuck in the back of my hand. Arguably, her husband got out of the dancing act more easily than I did.

Radio Waves and Waves on Radio

Radio was something very new during my boyhood, and Brother Frank went to work for CHNS, very close to where we lived—much to my parents' chagrin, I might add! They feared that this invention would erode the place of the piano as the home's entertainment centre. When I announced to my horror-stricken piano-making family that I was determined to be an actor, my father said, "My God, I don't know why you want to do that—we've got one bum in the family already!"

> *Radio had begun in Canada in Montreal in 1920. CHNS, Nova Scotia's first radio station, started broadcasting in 1926 from improvised studios in the Carleton Hotel, and later at the Lord Nelson Hotel. Radio was the new communication medium of Austin Willis's generation. It was less expensive than any previous communications technology, with early crystal sets not even requiring electricity. With few competing radio signals in the atmosphere, you could tune into signals hundreds of miles away, affording a broadening of horizons unthinkable for previous generations. No one even thought to regulate this new empowering medium until the Canadian Radio Broadcasting Commission was created, when Austin Willis was about fifteen.*

After he calmed down, the other "bum," Brother Frank, interceded on my behalf. Indeed, Frank gave me my first job on radio. He was doing *Harbour Lights* at CHNS, and my job was to make the sound of waves. We had to improvise—and our cardboard tube filled with buckshot sounded more like fire the first time we used it. You had to roll the tube just right for it to sound like waves.

Austin Willis beginning his career in radio at CHNS, *circa 1936.*

I was determined to work in radio, and I expected Brother Frank to find me *something* to do. ▢ I complained often and bitterly to our mother that he wouldn't let me on any of the radio shows he was organizing. Finally, the poor man submitted to this nagging and gave me a part. I picked up the script from his office and I looked up the name he had given me: "Morgan." Morgan had one line.

I went to Brother Frank and said, "Have I got this right—I have one line?" He said, "I know, I know—but throughout the whole script they talk about you—you're the heavy, you're the villain."

The radio program Harbour Lights, *with Marjorie Payne playing the organ, evolved to become* Atlantic Nocturne, *with J. Frank Willis reading poetry about the sea. It continued through to the 1950s from Toronto on* CBC *Radio.*

I relented. The line was: "I have come for the rent."
My first drama! My first radio acting job! It came my turn, I got the cue, said the line, and...my voice broke. I was convinced I had ruined his show, possibly his career. Fortunately, I hadn't.

It was undoubtedly Brother Frank's stature, if not his direct influence, that got me a job at CHNS as an announcer broadcasting from the top of the Lord Nelson Hotel. The CBC was located at the top of the Nova Scotian Hotel, and we pretended to be competitors, at least on air. ▢

Most Canadian radio stations began life inside hotels because the hotels invariably had ballrooms or venues that could easily be organized for live broadcast. Prominent visitors staying there could also be conveniently cajoled into doing live interviews.

My salary was a grand total of twelve dollars a week, but I also had a singalong thing with children at the Orpheus Theatre on Barrington Street every Saturday morning, sponsored by Farmer's Dairy—which handsomely supplemented that weekly wage.

Halifax was on the edge of the world in those days, and it was a great place to be. I sailed on the original *Bluenose* when she raced. ▢ And once, when I was working at CHNS, I nearly sank a submarine! We had a fellow from Boston bring a submarine into the harbour, and I convinced Major Borrett to let me go aboard and interview him on location. ▢

Bluenose is Nova Scotia's most famous sailing schooner, winning international races in the 1920s and 1930s. The image of Bluenose adorns the Canadian ten-cent piece, while its name is affectionately used as an appellation for all citizens of Nova Scotia—"Bluenosers."

W. C. Borrett was a soldier and radio signal operator in the First World War who founded CHNS after the war. He is best remembered for his own program, Tales Told from Under the Old Town Clock.

The fellow I was interviewing was a real grunter. I would ask him a big long question and he would simply grunt in response. Out of desperation I pulled a lever to see what would happen, and all of a sudden there was water coming into the submarine. He swore at me—on air—and ran up the ladder to remedy my mistake. I nearly lost my twelve dollars on that little go.

At the time, W. H. Brodie was travelling the country recruiting announcers for the CBC, and he approached me while I was working in Halifax. The CBC offered me $125 a month to go to Toronto, which was less than I was making in Halifax with all the commercials that earned me extra cash. I was having a great time in my hometown and didn't want to leave. But Brother Frank challenged me not to be content with being a big frog in a little puddle—but rather to try my hand in a bigger world. ⌐

> W. H. Brodie was a former English teacher who became coach, mentor, and eventually, controller of CBC announce staff, issuing weekly bulletins outlining the correct language and expression expected of CBC announcers.

TWO

Going to Toronto—
and Going to War

O nce I got to Toronto I immediately got myself into radio drama, as this new world offered dozens of possibilities in those days. Everything the CBC sent to any competition invariably won, and it was very difficult to get in as a young, relatively inexperienced actor.

Radio drama was also terrifying because it was broadcast live in those days—but at least we had our scripts in front of us. In rehearsal, directors would get you to do a scene over and over again. You would often do things you didn't know you could do.

An actor named John Drainie gave me advice one day that I have never forgotten. We were

The CBC's precursor, the Canadian Radio Broadcasting Commission, operated from 1932 to 1936 and had been inventing radio drama; it hired director Tyrone Guthrie from England, who went on to found the Stratford Festival of Canada. The 1938 US broadcast of Orson Welles's War of the Worlds demonstrated just how powerful radio drama could be.

rehearsing a fight scene, and I knew I just wasn't getting it to sound right for radio. Drainie said, "Aust—you are not making any pictures. For every word that I speak on radio I make pictures in my mind. It's in colour, and that seems to get it off the page."◻

> *John Drainie had begun his formidable radio acting career in Vancouver and in 1943 moved to Toronto, where he was soon considered Canada's leading radio drama actor. Orson Welles called him "the greatest radio actor in the world."*

How I Started the Second World War

Shortly after I moved to Toronto to work for CBC Radio, I got blamed for starting the war.

CBL was the "anchor" station for the network, because we broadcast news to the whole country. One day, I happened to be sitting in the CBL booth as we were playing "Smoke Gets in your Eyes." Someone came running in wild-eyed from the newsroom and handed me a piece of paper. I broke in and said, "Ladies and gentlemen: I interrupt this program and bring you a special bulletin—Canada has declared war on Nazi Germany."

As required when announcing a bulletin of this importance, I read it a second time.

"Ladies and gentlemen: I interrupt this program and bring you a special bulletin—Canada has declared war on Nazi Germany."

After making this grave declaration, I returned to regular programming. On this day, unfortunately, it meant listeners digesting the ominous news were served up an utterly ridiculous but popular novelty tune: "Inka Dinka Doo."◻

> *With reference to the "Inka Dinka Doo" incident, the* Financial Post *later reported that "incredible stupidity had been shown by Canada's state-owned broadcasting... with no sense of the sober gravity" that the announcement warranted.*

From that time on, I appeared in books as having started the war.

Then along came Lorne Greene, who became known as the "Voice of Doom," because the early part of the war was an unrelenting litany of bad and tragic news, with all the bombing and destruction in Britain and the loss of ships at sea.

Lorne Greene was the principal news reader in the early days of the CBC. A trained actor, his distinctively deep, resonant voice was also heard on early NFB documentaries about the war.

When Lorne came into his booth adjacent to mine, he would wave his announcer's script, typed on yellow paper. I would wait until he got seated and then interrupt the program to allow him to read the latest bulletin. One day, he reported on the loss of two British ships in the Indian Ocean, with a catastrophic loss of life. I sat there stunned by this tragedy until the dead silence indicated Lorne had finished and I had to get back on air immediately.

In those days on CBC Radio, we not only made service announcements but had to do commercials as well. I flipped open the folder, switched on my microphone, and read the first commercial in the pile: "Ladies and gentlemen, get your son in the service a Bulova watch; they are watertight!"

The phone rang almost instantly in the booth. The voice was one I knew only too well. Brother Frank had been listening to the radio in his office. "What a wonderful placement for that spot, Aust! You might have done the sponsor an ill service, though, as I wouldn't think anyone would want to buy a Bulova watch after that."

I was devastated about that (and decades later, I still am, a bit). I died for the next six months. I must have been interviewed by eleven different CBC executives. Even after the war, every time John Drainie passed me in the hallway, he would just say, "Gurgle, gurgle, gurgle." I was treated like an outcast—and deservedly so, I must say.

While working at the CBC in Toronto, we were told we were necessary in the war effort and would be protected from conscription if it was instituted. I had come from Nova Scotia and knew a lot of people in the navy, especially in the officer corps,

Austin Willis volunteered to join the Royal Canadian Navy in 1941.

because of my involvement with them in the Theatre Arts Guild. As the war went on, I became more interested in joining the service, so I went down one day to the volunteer recruitment centre at HMCS *York* in the automotive building on the exhibition grounds. If I could qualify, I wanted to be an officer. I had heard that the selection board was coming through and that's how they chose officers: you went before them and if they thought you were suitable, they would put you into training. I was accepted to go before the selection board.

When the time came, I sat outside waiting. I remember that day so well because it struck me that for someone who aspired to be an officer, I had the wrong clothing on—a plaid suit. I thought, "Oh dear, this is not stately enough."

It worried me greatly that they would turn me down because of my inappropriate suit. And then, when I walked in the room, I knew half the people at the table! They were from Halifax. They didn't want to talk to me—they all wanted to know how Brother Frank was doing. I got through the interview and went away to wait. Finally, I heard I'd been chosen for officer training, but then there was a long time before I was actually "called up." They eventually did call for me, and I was to be sent for training at King's College in Halifax. I was more than ready, but when I got to Halifax, I received a telegram—a "flimsy," as they called it—ordering me to report instead to Ottawa to Naval Information as quickly as possible. ▢

Austin Willis so treasured his navy uniform that he carefully kept his officer's hat and jacket for many years, eventually including them as part of his donation to the Saint Mary's University Archives.

Ducks, Banjos, Hockey Rinks, and Celebrities

To my disappointment, I ended up back in the radio business, hosting the *Victory Loan Hour* that I had already been doing—just now in a different suit. I was much chagrined and very angry at this turn of events. Certainly, it was not the plan I'd had when I enlisted.

These shows were performed in front of live audiences, often at Massey Hall in Toronto, and always to a full house. I did four shows a year, three months apart, for three years. I started off dressed in a tailcoat and wound up dressed in a navy uniform. We would also enact small dramas, which I might narrate, depicting some adventure to show what war was like. The *Victory Loan* shows were also performed at theatres in Ottawa and Montreal. Afterwards, for a week or two, we would tour factories and service spaces with some real stars—and boy, what stars they were.

The shows were done for a cause I completely believed in, and the biggest names in movies came to Canada. Clark Gable, Gary Cooper, Spencer Tracy, Ronald Colman, Bob Hope, James Cagney, Humphrey Bogart, Joan Crawford, Norma Shearer, Betty Grable, Greer Garson, Ingrid Bergman, Ralph Bellamy, and many others. The music was directed by Percy Faith. Lorne Greene did the commercials. The shows were just marvellous, and it was very exciting to be the master of ceremonies for all this—particularly in my mid-twenties.

Mind you, we had some glitches. One night I remember in particular involved British film actor Ronald Colman and American actor Clarence Nash.[⌑] Nash, who was the voice of Donald Duck, worked with a white duck that he would hold facing the audience. As he spoke, you would swear the duck was speaking—Nash, as it turned out, was a very skilled ventriloquist. It was an amazingly entertaining act. Next I introduced Ronald Colman, but Colman didn't come out from behind the curtain. Rather, that bloody white duck did! The audience in the theatre fell out of their seats

Ronald Colman was a British-born actor who became a leading man in Hollywood in the 1920s. Clarence Nash was an American voice actor, best known as the original voice of the Disney cartoon character Donald Duck.

laughing—but the audience listening at home wondered if Ronald Colman had come out without his trousers or something, or whether I had done something dreadful.

Eddie Peabody was born in Massachusetts and made his reputation playing in vaudeville in the 1920s. During the Second World War he performed widely for servicemen.

Another time we had Eddie Peabody, considered to be the greatest banjo player in the world. I always thought a banjo was a banjo was a banjo, but Peabody made one sound like it was a classical instrument—like a whole orchestra.

There was also a wonderful actress on the bill whose name I won't mention. She was cranky and complained about everything. She didn't like her hotel suite, she didn't like the food—she was just plain unhappy about everything and made a point of expressing all her discontents in a great loud voice. We weren't used to that kind of behaviour. The other Hollywood people were true professionals—they never complained about anything.

We were busy coping with our various duties on the program, and this actress wanted to introduce Eddie Peabody. I was dying to introduce him, but the actress insisted on doing it because she thought he was so great. She was very charming, very witty, and very gracious with Eddie—and ended her introduction by saying, "Ladies and gentlemen, Mr. Playbody will now pee for you."

Before I went overseas, I hosted the *Hot Stove League*—the chatter between periods of the NHL hockey games being broadcast from Maple Leaf Gardens. I wasn't there for my expertise in hockey, but rather because I was known to any celebrities who might have been visiting town. I remember once taking George

George Raft was the consummate gangster in Hollywood crime melodramas of the 1930s and 1940s.

Raft up to the press gondola that was suspended high above the ice at Maple Leaf Gardens to watch the game after we had done our interview in our basement studio. He literally froze in fear on the narrow catwalk that led to the gondola—and we had a devil of a time getting him down from there.

Out of the Booth and Into Uniform

I finally got to London in 1944—the time of the dreaded "buzz bomb." I was to report to the Canadian Naval Mission Overseas (CNMO). I walked down to their location in the Haymarket and followed the signs upstairs for the Canadian Navy. When I got up there, carrying my bags and luggage, I couldn't find a soul in the office. Suddenly a voice said, "Get down you fool!" It was Bob Shuttleworth, an orchestra leader who had joined the navy, but he was under a table, as was everybody else in the office.

I noticed the sound of a motor going but didn't realize it was a buzz bomb—I had never heard one before. Suddenly the thing went off somewhere—BOOM!—and where seconds ago there had been nobody, the office was now filled with people who'd emerged from under their desks. Everyone was so terrified of this new weapon that whenever they heard one, they automatically dove for cover.

Stanley Maxted was a well-known Canadian broadcaster and singer who had gone overseas before the war and had been very successful with the start of commercial radio in England. He was accredited to the BBC and, of course, I knew him very well. We often linked up together in getting stories, bringing them back to London, and broadcasting them home.

Stanley Maxted was the British counterpart to the CBC's Matthew Halton—a respected journalist and war correspondent—visiting the troops in action and reporting on radio throughout the war.

One time in Brixham, Maxted and I took a torpedo boat crewed by a bunch of Canadians to a

British battleship in the harbour. As were climbing aboard the big ship, she fired her guns...and shot her own observation plane out of the air! Everyone on the ship was terribly upset, and it was clearly no place to be for the next while, so we turned around and left—we were not going to accomplish anything there.

Later, in September 1944, I was out in the torpedo boats when they were chasing u-boats. As an officer, I was required to carry a gun—a huge Colt .44 that weighed a ton. If you didn't carry it, a superior office would say, "Where's your gun?" and you'd better have one to show him.

Anyway, I got so excited that I pulled out this damn pistol I had been lugging around forever and started firing at the u-boats, which were three or four miles away. There was no chance of a bullet getting anywhere near the enemy. Our commander said, "Oh, Austin—please leave some for us!"

I then realized exactly how stupid I must have looked and quickly holstered the pistol. It was the first, last, and only time I ever fired that gun.

To Jump or Not To Jump

The war was winding down and Stanley Maxted invited me to join him in reporting on the battles at Arnhem in the Netherlands. We were to be parachuted into Arnhem where the fighting really was furious. Before we could do this, we had to go to Brixham to learn how to jump out of a plane.

Two days later we're sitting in a plane with parachutes on. There's a wire that runs along the length of the plane, and when the green light comes on, you jump, and this wire pulls your parachute open. Maxted pats my knee, says, "We'll see you on the ground!" and jumps out the door.

The American sergeant beckons me with his hand. I get up, walk over, take hold of the side of the door like the others, and wait. The light comes on and...no way am I going to let go of the sides of the door. The sergeant pushes me a bit—not too hard.

He couldn't have moved me with a Sherman tank, so he just pulled me back. When he did, I let go of the door and sat down. I wanted to jump very much, but there was no going to Arnhem for me; my body simply wouldn't let me.

Stanley Maxted was later captured and held behind enemy lines at Arnhem, where he made secret recordings on a disc recorder that were eventually broadcast by the BBC and CBC.

My wartime service was definitely not distinguished—though I did keep my Colt .44 with me all these years. It is with the memorabilia from my life at the Saint Mary's University Archives. I trust that they have disarmed it by now.

Years later, when living outside Edmonton, Austin Willis did a series of interviews with veterans called Comrades in Arms *for Veterans Affairs.* Comrades in Arms *was produced by the Video Production Unit of Veterans Affairs in the 1990s for potential broadcast on community cable stations. Copies are held in the Austin Willis collection at the Saint Mary's University Archives in Halifax.*

THREE

Inventing a Film Industry
for Canada—or Trying to

adio was my first career, but I always wanted to do more. After the war, two friends of mine—Larry Cromien from the air force and Gordon Burwash, another navy fellow—and I pooled our "go home" money together and decided to make a movie. We got together with another Canadian aviator who'd served in both wars, Sterling Campbell, who had some experience in Hollywood, and he became our director.▢

Campbell formed a company, Dominion Productions, which we expected to become *the* Canadian film production enterprise. We also interested G. H. Wood (his "Sanitation for the Nation" company made paper cups, liquid soap, and commercial cleaning products) in financing our

> Sterling Campbell served in the Royal Canadian Army during the First World War and in the Royal Canadian Air Force during the Second World War, and worked in Hollywood as an assistant director between the wars.

venture, eventually putting together $150,000 to make a movie called *Bush Pilot*.

I had a very good friend in Hollywood, an actor called Ralph Bellamy, and I sought out his advice.◻ I told him we were going to make *Bush Pilot* and that it was going to be a B picture. He said, "Stop right there! That's what you should never do—make a B picture.... If you intend to make any money and if you intend to do anything that is worthwhile, you should be making an A movie."

I said that was all we could afford to do. He said, "Okay, I have done my duty—so let's get on with it."

We got Scott Darling, then working in Hollywood, to write us a script.◻ Bellamy found two established American actors, Jack La Rue and Rochelle Hudson—who used up most of our budget.◻ We believed that this would guarantee us American distribution for our movie.

I was also the casting director, and I chose a young actor named Frank Perry, instead of Bob Goulet, to play my brother. In my opinion at that time, Goulet was never going to go anywhere. (Was I wrong!)◻

Ralph Bellamy was an American actor of stage, screen, and television who was also head of Actors' Equity in New York. Years later, in the 1960s, he played President Franklin D. Roosevelt in Sunrise at Campobello *and had a guest role in the* CBC *series* Seaway, *led by Austin Willis. Bellamy eventually received an Honorary Academy Award in 1986.*

Scott Darling was a Toronto-born writer who worked in Hollywood from 1914 to 1951, writing dozens of scripts for major films and B movie thrillers.

Jack La Rue was a New Yorker who first acted on Broadway and then in Hollywood; he had roles in more than a hundred films. Rochelle Hudson was a well-known Hollywood actress who invariably played the love interest of lead actors from the 1930s to the 1960s.

Frank Perry was a Toronto-born actor who had a successful career in film and television after Bush Pilot. *Robert Goulet was born in America to French-Canadian parents; he eventually became a well-known singer on stage and screen.*

Before his hair turned silver, Austin Willis invested and starred in Bush Pilot, *1946.*

We shot all of our outdoor footage in Muskoka, and I remember giving La Rue the script when he arrived. He only wanted his "side"—just the pages with his lines. Jack said, "I never read the whole script—I don't want to spoil the picture for myself when I see it." Jack La Rue made dozens of pictures but never saw any of them until they were complete.

Rochelle Hudson was our other lead, opposite me, and we needed a train for a scene in which her character was leaving mine. We were spending our money very expeditiously and approached officials at the Canadian National Railway (CNR) but couldn't afford their fees—so we went down to the station and waited most of the day for the Canadian Pacific Railway (CPR) train to arrive so we could get the scene. Their trains were certainly not running on a movie schedule, but a train did finally turn up—and we got the shot, which lasted about thirty seconds in the movie.

Then, on our second day, we were going to do a big fight scene on the docks between me and La Rue. La Rue was expecting body doubles to do the close-ups, and I had to explain to him that we had no money for doubles. He said, "I've done a million fights in movies. I'll teach Austin how to do it."

I was quite willing to learn. We started off and the first punch I threw hit La Rue right in the throat. Blood shot out of his mouth and I thought I had killed him! He sank down and fell off the pier into the water—and was off the picture for four days. We had planned to have half the picture finished in those four days. That cost us a fortune.

The cast of Bush Pilot, *1946. Austin Willis is fourth from the left.*

When he returned, we were going to stage the fight again. Now I was missing him by three feet every time! That's why the fight looks as staged as it does. The story of that fight actually got back to Hollywood, and years later when I got out there people would smile and say, "I heard you had a great fight with Jack La Rue."

For our aerial footage in *Bush Pilot*, we had another fellow from Hollywood who said he knew all about shooting from the air. All the scenes where you see either me or La Rue in a plane were shot in a studio in Montreal in a mock-up in front of a screen with the sky moving behind us. Afterward, the crew took the two planes we had hired and shot footage from the airplanes as they were in flight.

When we saw the rushes everything was beautiful—with one glitch.

In the mock-up shots, we were flying from screen left to screen right, but all the stuff in the air was shot with the action moving from screen right to screen left. When they cut the footage together, Jack La Rue was chasing me in his airplane, but his clouds were travelling with him. The editors tried to correct this, but it looks like I don't know in which direction I am flying. We had a very quick meeting and decided we couldn't afford to bring the planes back. We had to send our footage to a specialty lab in Hollywood, where they took the negative and turned it over. The planes were finally flying in the same direction as the mock-up. The only problem was that all the lettering on my plane was now backwards—and it looked like the Russian air force. We had to limit our use of our aerial shots in the final film.

We held the premiere of *Bush Pilot* in Montreal in 1947. When I saw it, I wasn't displeased with it. I thought that, for a country that didn't make motion pictures, we had done well. We had raised the money; we had used a local crew. If you see it now I believe

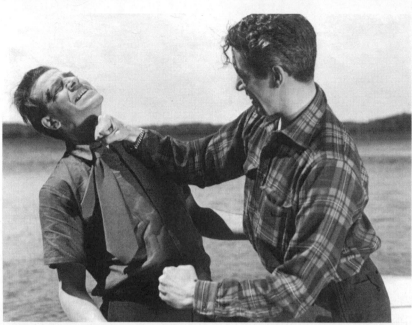

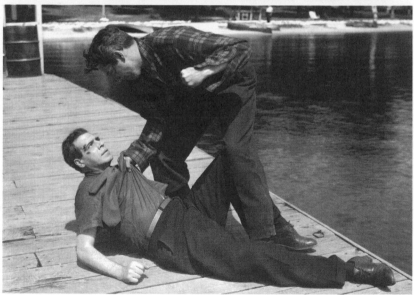

TOP AND BOTTOM: *Austin Willis (in plaid) and Jack La Rue slug it out in* Bush Pilot, 1946.

that it stands up well, considering when it was made and the
money we had.🎞

But whether *Bush Pilot* made
money or not, I don't know. I
sold my stock the night of our
premiere, and I got my invest-
ment back and more, but we couldn't get an American distributor. It should have done very well with Jack La Rue and Rochelle
Hudson, but America wouldn't let us in.

Bush Pilot *was never distributed*
outside Canada. The negative was
deposited at the Public Archives
of Canada in 1972 and has since
been restored; it can now be seen on
YouTube.

The Wages, and Litigation, of Sin

Five days later, Larry Cromien arrived and said, "We are going to
do another picture."

He told me the whole plan for *Sins of the Fathers*. A movie had
recently been released in the us called *Mom and Dad*; it explored
sexual misadventures and the consequences of casual sex.🎞

The filmmakers would go into movie theatres and do one showing a day, then have someone speak after the screening. My partner
with *Bush Pilot* suggested that we
were going to do the same with
a movie called *Sins of the Fathers*.

I was looking forward to a
career in the movies, on stage, in
lovely comedies—and was having
great fun. I certainly wasn't seek-
ing controversy, but I allowed
myself to be talked into it, and I
found myself back in Montreal to
shoot *Sins of the Fathers*.

Basically, we got films about
venereal disease from the army,

Mom and Dad, *also known as*
The Family Story, *was a highly*
controversial 1945 American film
denounced for its candid representation
of sexuality, presented under the guise
of educational content. It was made
on a $63,000 budget and grossed an
estimated $50 million, prompting
many imitations. It led to more than
four hundred lawsuits that sought to
have the film censored. It has since been
added to the American National Film
Registry.

navy, and air force and made a movie around them. I played Doctor Ben, and Joy Lafleur played the afflicted lady. My role was to scold her while showing her these movies on the ravages of venereal disease.▫

Joy Lafleur was a Montreal actress whose first film was Sins of the Fathers; *she went on to have a brief career in Hollywood and died at the age of forty-three.*

The Royal Alexandra Theatre was built in 1907 and is the oldest continuously operating theatre in North America.

We opened in 1948 at the Royal Alexandra Theatre in Toronto, a very staid old theatre.▫ I had done some stage work there and the manager knew me personally, which was the only reason he allowed *Sins of the Fathers* into his very plush, stately theatre. Because of the nature of its content, audiences were segregated: a men's performance was shown in the afternoon and a women's performance in the evening, or vice-versa—a different sequence on alternating days.

Austin Willis and Joy Lafleur in Sins of the Fathers, *1948.*

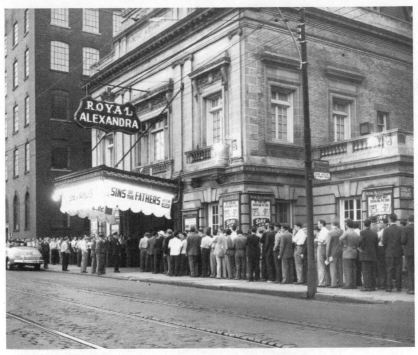

Crowds lined up at the Royal Alexandra Theatre in Toronto to see Sins of the Fathers *in 1948.*

After the screening, an old friend, actor Sydney Brown (whom we called a "sexologist"), came out on stage with a book that we had printed. We showed stills from the picture and had Syd present a commentary, saying what the audience should do to prevent getting venereal disease. He came out unabashedly, as though he were a doctor, gave this long speech, and sold these books. We made more money from these books than from the people coming in the doors (admittance was seventy-five cents, and the book cost a dollar).

The first afternoon was a men's performance, and the crowd trying to get into the theatre went right around the block. There was no chance that half of the people were going to get in. They pulled the doors right off their hinges. The manager of the Royal

Alex was in the middle of the lobby having a stroke—here was this lovely regal theatre being torn to shreds before his eyes.

On the first night, we were all at the back of the theatre—the old partners from *Bush Pilot*—standing there wondering what was going to happen. We didn't know if the audience liked it or not, because there was no laughter. There was no applause. The silence was scary.

Our dramatization ended and the medical films came on. They consisted mostly of close-ups of needles being pushed into people's arms. As we were watching the screen (which was very white, as the medical men wore white coats) people silhouetted against it started standing up and then instantly falling to the floor. When the lights went up, the floor was strewn with bodies—people who had fainted when a needle pierced someone's skin onscreen. We had no medical help in the theatre for this—just

Austin Willis as Doctor Ben in Sins of the Fathers, *1948.*

three ushers. From then on, we got the St. John Ambulance corps to attend every performance.

We played to packed houses during the week. We couldn't have jammed another body in there. At the end of the week we were in rhapsody and delight about the success that this was obviously going to have wherever we showed it.

Come Saturday night, we were in the manager's office splitting up the spoils from the box office for the week: half went to us and our backers; the other half went to our distributor. Then I asked, "What about the book now?"

Our distributor insisted that the book was his. The backers got up and nearly choked him to death right on the spot. There was litigation the next day. By the time the litigation settled a year later, the idea and the picture were gone. Thus ended the sad story of *Sins of the Fathers*.

FOUR

Doing Everything and Anything on Radio

D uring the war, I had tried my hand at some reporting in England, but it didn't come naturally to me. I loved Great Britain, though, particularly London, and found myself another radio venture when the play *Detective Story*, in which I was appearing, closed after two weeks in 1950. I had rented an apartment for six months and was desperately looking around the city for work. I called on my old refuge, the CBC, and contacted a dear man, Harry Boyle, who was running the corporation in those days.

> *Harry J. Boyle worked for CBC Radio in Toronto from 1942 until 1968 and thereafter with the CRTC until 1977. He is fondly remembered by dozens of writers and performers, and millions of Canadians, for making CBC Radio the link that held the country together.*

I asked him for help. Boyle invited me to help him create a documentary series about England; he was confident I'd find interesting topics to pursue. This was very complimentary, I thought, so away I went and dreamed up an idea for a series that explored things that interested me in Britain—classic stories, and questions such as: Was there really a Loch Ness monster? Were there really any pirates of Penzance? And so on.

I had friends who owned a rare Bristol automobile, and they proposed to take me along on their tour of England. I would interview people and record these interview on discs, which I would then take back to the BBC. I'd read my story at the BBC studio and they would transmit it across the Atlantic via shortwave, just like we had done during the war.

Fortunately, I kept the scripts. When I went back to Toronto, they hadn't yet broadcast the series, so we re-recorded the whole thing to get better sound quality than the shortwave transmissions. We called my series *Glimpses of Britain*, and this began my storytelling career on radio.

When I got back to Toronto, I started doing a ninety-minute daily show on CBC Radio entitled *Of All Things*, on whatever inspired me—whether it was reading poetry, playing recorded music, or telling stories. It ran for twelve years. I was a freelancer in those days, and eventually I also told stories on a series

A postcard promoting Matinée with Willis, *1959*

called *Matinée with Willis*, which was heard on private radio stations across the country. This eventually evolved into *Stories to Remember* in 1966—historical tales told in the run-up to Canada's centennial in 1967.

And yes—I represented the show's sponsor, Matinée cigarettes. I feel very guilty about this now! We did the show from

Austin Willis represented Matinée cigarettes, as shown in this 1962 magazine ad.

various radio stations, often with live audiences, and one day I asked the Matinée representative who was travelling with us whether I needed to mention the sponsor. He assured me that I didn't need to, as I always had a cigarette in my hand—which was the best endorsement they could ask for. But these were also the folks who sponsored my 1963 speaking tour across the country promoting a national theatre for Canada—and that was a cultural institution I very much believed in.

More Than "Just" Mary

I did everything and anything on radio. One of my favourite things was working with Mary Grannan. She arrived in Toronto the same year I did—a fellow Maritimer and a former teacher from Fredericton—and she was a great friend of Brother Frank's. [□]

I was her announcer on *Just Mary*, a show for children aged four to eight, which Mary had begun at CFNB in Fredericton before she came to the CBC. We would be in adjoining booths where we could signal to each other through the glass. After introducing her, I would get out my fingernail file and start to file my nails while listening.

We had been doing the show together for about six months when she got a new young producer. Well, when the program was over, this guy turned to me and tore a strip off me for at least twenty minutes. I thought he was going to have a heart attack! He yelled that I was showing no respect for the artistry of the performer and that it was simply hideous to take out a fingernail file and clean my nails. As the

Mary Grannan was an award-winning writer of children's stories. Just Mary: The Life of Mary Evelyn Grannan, *published by Dundurn Press in 2006 and written by Margaret Anne Hume, includes extensive interviews with Austin Willis. On March 27, 2018, Mary Grannan was designated a National Historic Person by Parks Canada.*

fellow ranted on, I was cringing more and more. Then Mary—bless her—tore a strip off him that lasted equally long! She said: "How *dare* you speak to Mr. Willis like that! If he didn't file his fingernails, he would not be listening, and I would be very upset. I love him filing his fingernails. It is wonderful, and it inspires me!"

There was never another peep from that producer.

Mary invented names for her favourite CBC people, and I was "Austy the Alligator," who was quite a mean character. "Frankie Frankfurter" was my brother. She then went on to do the *Children's Scrapbook* for slightly older children, and she practically wrote the show for me. She wanted me to be Master of

Mary Grannan (centre right) wearing her signature black hat, and Austin Willis (left) at CBC circa 1940s.

Ceremonies, but I was also a character. It was all bits and pieces of whatever occurred to her that might engage children—sometimes poetry, sometimes little acted-out shows, sometimes visits to workplaces.

"Where are we going today, Austin?" she would ask, and I would reply, "Well, I'm going to take you to a barn to see a lovely bunch of cows."

And off we'd go to a farm. These segments would be pre-recorded on actual locations outside the studio. Mary had a vivid, vivid imagination. She would go off on flights of fancy and take the kids who were listening at home along with her. That's why they loved her.

While I was showing children around the farm, dramatic things would happen to me. I'd fall down in the mud. I'd get into terrible trouble with a bull. I'd have to shuffle the children out of harm's way. This was to illustrate farm life to kids. But the theme changed every week, subject to Mary's creative imagination.

Not Exactly Everybody's Cup of Tea

Those were great years in radio, and I have to tell you about Henrietta Ball—*the* head of publicity at CBC for ages and ages. "Henri" Ball was a remarkable woman. She held Sunday soirees—tea parties, actually—at her apartment in Rosedale, and you were not really *in* the CBC unless you were invited to one of these things. If you were invited, you'd better show up, because "not to go was a no-no."

We were all a little afraid of Henri, who was a big, tall lady—handsome was the word—not pretty, but handsome. Her tea parties were interminable. There was never a drop of alcohol—it was frowned upon. So guys like Percy Faith and Stanley Maxted would smuggle in a twenty-six-ouncer of rye, lift the back of the toilet, and stow it in the water tank. ▢ Then, after every few cups of tea, they'd get up and say: "Well, I have to go to the bathroom because of all this." They'd head off and have a good sip of rye.

And of course, some would get very merry by the end of the tea party. Henrietta could never figure out where they got the booze.

Maybe those tea parties are where I got my appetite for strong drink—which sometimes did not serve me well in the years to come.

Percy Faith was a Toronto-born musician, composer, arranger, and orchestra leader who became well-known and appreciated in the US for his popular music, including such hits as the Grammy-winning "Theme from A Summer Place." He's considered by many to be the originator of "easy listening music."

FIVE

Inventing Television— or Trying to

T he Brits and the Americans both had television, but their systems employed different technical standards and Canada had to decide which one to adopt.[□] That was the big question. The CBC sent Mavor Moore to London and Brother Frank to New York to do some investigating.

> Television technologies were being developed in England, Japan, Hungary, Russia, Germany, and the United States from 1897 to the 1930s, with national broadcasting beginning in the 1940s. Different technical standards were developed in different countries. Canadians living close enough to the American border to receive a signal started watching US television in the 1940s. In September 1952 the CBC began national television broadcasting from Toronto and Montreal using the American "525-line" system.

Mavor was in London for two weeks and Brother Frank was in New York for three.☐ Brother Frank told me that he got a huge bottle of rye and a comfortable hotel room. He went see NBC first, to look at their studios and their shows. Then he went back to his hotel, got into bed, opened the bottle of rye—and never got out of bed again during that visit. Both he and Mavor wrote reports about what they had discovered. The CBC chose Brother Frank's advice to go the way the Americans had gone because it would have been more complicated to adopt the British system.☐

Mavor Moore was a Toronto-born actor, producer, and writer; he was the CBC's first chief producer, and he considered himself the first employee of CBC Television.

The CBC was on Jarvis Street in Toronto in what was the old Havergal College, the former girls' school. It had been condemned before the war and was standing empty. As the war continued and programs grew in number, the CBC occupied more and more of the abandoned building. When television came along, the CBC stayed there, contributing an addition with a television studio in the parking lot. Next to that, they put up a huge television transmitter.

Historians now concede that Canada waited so long to adopt a television format that we had to follow the American standard—because so many Canadians already had televisions and were expecting American technology and programming.

The day I walked across the parking lot into the new building, my life changed.

Avoid the Cables If You're Able

Early TV was a madhouse. For the actor it was hell! He was thrown into a small room full of scenery—scenery nailed to the floor, scenery on wheels, and scenery hanging by ropes from the ceiling. He faced three or four cameras that whizzed around what was left of the floor space like angry monsters. As well as learning what he had to say, he had to also learn which of four thousand marks on the floor he was expected to stand on at different times. He had to learn to walk to all these marks and hit them dead-on without looking down at them. He had to stand so close to his colleagues that much of his salary went to Odorono antiperspirant and Lavoris mouthwash! And he had to learn to act with his left eyeball only, as that was the main part of him seen through the entire show!

There we were, with a billion-dollar toy, and none of us knew how to use it. We would rehearse in a studio with the set painted on the floor, and then we would rehearse with the sets in place for one day, with the show being broadcast live the next day. This gave us one day to get used to the actual scenery, the camera, the lights, and all the people running around doing their jobs. You hoped you could remember your lines and get through it. The cameras were enormous, and the floors were covered with cables three inches thick. All the technicians were as nervous as we were about this new medium. They whispered to each other constantly. As an actor you just hoped you could remember your lines and somehow get through it.

In one scene, I was supposed to share a kiss with a British actress. The cameras came in close for our kiss while huge, heavy cables were being pulled under our feet. It was not a very convincing kiss! The audience at home must have wondered what was going on. I'm glad I never saw myself in that program—and indeed I have rarely seen myself in anything from that first decade of television.

I was interviewed more than once by Elwood Glover on the CBC daily television show *Luncheon Date*, which was broadcast live

> Early television was live, with film only used for newsgathering or for making kinescopes of programs that were filmed as they were being broadcast and then shipped across the country for rebroadcasting.

from the lobby of the Four Seasons Hotel in Toronto.▢ He would "pretend" to interrupt me as I was walking through the Four Seasons Hotel lobby on Jarvis Street and sit me down for an impromptu interview. With Elwood, I would usually end up interviewing him.

Austin Willis interviewing, or being interviewed by, Elwood Glover on Luncheon Date, *1965.*

Commanding Space

My first role in television was as the commander on a show called *Space Command*. It was a children's series written by Alf Harris and produced by Murray Chercover.▢

Jimmy Doohan was my space-travelling lieutenant, and William Shatner would later succeed me as commander.⊞ We had many others on the show who went on to have storied careers in television—including Norman Jewison, who was our cable-puller.⊞ I have always considered *Space Command* the forerunner to *Star Trek*—though I doubt that anyone else does.⊞

For *Space Command* they put up a big black curtain on one wall of the studio and attached sparkly things from the nearest dime store to it. On camera it looked remarkably like a sky. The suits we wore were made of felt! Maybe somebody had to get rid of a whole lot of felt? What was in their minds, making costumes of felt? The lights were bad enough, but with those felt costumes you'd lose ten pounds at a go.

They hired me because I had white hair. My role as Earthbound commander was set in an office, where I would talk to a dozen spaceships, all by number.

"Spaceship 207, are you in Orbit 12 or Orbit 14?"

I couldn't keep track, so I left pieces of paper around so I could sneak a look and keep the

James Doohan was born in British Columbia and had dozens of roles in Canadian radio and television before becoming "Scotty" on Star Trek. *William Shatner was born in Montreal, acting onstage in Ottawa and Stratford and appearing in a variety of* CBC Television *series' in the early 1950s before moving to Hollywood. His blustery style created his brand as Captain Kirk on* Star Trek.

Norman Jewison was born in Toronto; after serving with the Royal Canadian Navy in the Second World War, he began his career with CBC Television *in 1952. He went on to become a celebrated director and producer, and was later nominated for Best Director Academy Awards for* In the Heat of the Night, Fiddler on the Roof, *and* Moonstruck.

Star Trek *debuted on* NBC *television in 1966 with William Shatner as captain of the space ship* USS Enterprise; *the show ran until 1969.* Star Trek *was revived in feature films in the 1970s and 1980s and then returned to television— becoming one of the most successful media enterprises and influences on popular culture of all time.*

numbers straight. We would do the dress rehearsal and it would go fine, but then they would clean up the studio for the final show—and all my notes would disappear. So I would make up numbers as I went along, and the other actors never knew what or when to reply—throwing the whole thing into terrible confusion some nights.

For spacewalks we had a sawhorse on wheels, draped in the same black velvet as the back wall. They had a rope tied to the front of it and would pull it across the set—and you would swear the guy was flying around in space. Jimmy Doohan was always doing spacewalks; he had a contraption that he could squeeze that would send out puffs of white dust, making it look like he was propelling himself through space. One night Jimmy Doohan was doing his spacewalk on this contraption when I heard a groan, and I could see plainly that he was in trouble. He was slipping off the sawhorse on live television, so I got down on my hands and knees and crawled out on the floor and put my hand up to steady him. He whispered, "Thanks."

Space Command was the CBC's first dramatic series. It began in March of 1953; 150 episodes were produced and distributed across the country. Only the pilot has survived at the CBC Archives.

When I got home after that episode, the phone rang. Brother Frank was calling to say how much he enjoyed the show, especially the human hand in space with the Willis family ring!▢

Don't Get Hit on Hit Parade

My next role proved to be even more hazardous—though it looked safe enough. I was host of *Cross-Canada Hit Parade*—an obvious copy of the American *Your Hit Parade* show.▢

Your Hit Parade began on American radio in 1935 and on American television in 1950; it was sponsored by Lucky Strike cigarettes.

We needed dancers and we had a wonderful dance troupe in

Austin Willis commanding space on the set of Space Command, *circa 1953.*

Toronto—as good as any in New York City. Wally Koster led the orchestra, and Joyce Hahn was our regular singer. 🎞

We needed extras to be our audience on the show, sitting at tables or on benches. Joyce Hahn would sing to them whatever romantic ballad was on top of the chart that week. A great friend of mine, Bernie Slade, would be paid maybe fifty dollars, and all you could ever see was the back of his head in the

Wally Koster was a Winnipeg-born actor and singer who was very active in television, recording, and nightclubs in Toronto in the 1950s and 1960s. Joyce Hahn was born in Saskatoon and sang in a family troupe in the 1930s and 1940s, then performed in Montreal nightclubs and on CBC Television.

shot. Joyce apparently liked to sing to him. ᗯ

We had a different guest star every week; I would interview them, and then the orchestra and chorus would perform the hit songs of the time. One song I came to hate was called "The Green Door." We must have played that something like 122 times. ᗯ

For my introductions, I stood in front of a map of Canada that was maybe five feet across and hung one foot above my head. That was my set. If I didn't stand in front of it squarely, you could see what was happening on the set on either side of the map. It was also on wheels, and the echo of my voice would not even have died out before the map was whisked away. We were in a very small studio, and they changed the scenery, all on wheels, all very rapidly—you could get severely injured during scene changes. That was what concerned me—not my performance on air, but whether I would get away without being injured. ᗯ

Hypnotizing the Nation

On the Spot was a fifteen-minute show on CBC Television in those first years. It was about anything and everything and was hosted by Fred Davis. ᗯ

I was brought in on occasion to be the host when they believed that the topic would suit me. One week, they were having a hypnotist on, and he was going to hypnotize me on television. He had tried before

and couldn't. This time he asked me to bring something important to me. I brought my grandfather's watch. The hypnotist swung the watch back and forth and I followed it with my eyes; he followed it with his eyes. We had great shots of eyes on this show. He kept it up for five minutes, and I was still as wide awake as I would be at noon.

We laughed about it, and I apologized for not being hypnotized. When the show was off-air we sat in the studio and talked a bit before we finally went into the lobby. The lobby at the CBC in those days housed the reception desk and the telephone switchboard. Every line was plugged in at the switchboard, and it was lit up like a like a Christmas tree. Our receptionist/operator was standing there with her hands on her hips.

"You fellows are in trouble," she said. "You have hypnotized the whole country! What are you going to do about it?!"

After the national news aired, I got our hypnotist back on the air in a big rush. He waved the watch and told everyone to wake up. We didn't hear any more complaints and assumed that all was well—but that wasn't quite true.

One poor lady had continued hitting her husband with a magazine, pulling his hair, and slapping his face—and he still wasn't moving. She eventually called back to tell us that her husband had not been hypnotized—he was just dead!

SIX

On Stage—and Off

I'd always loved the theatre, so I returned to London, England, after the war. I thought that with this new medium of television looming, it would be great to get some serious acting experience on the stage as a way of preparing myself to act on television. People go to the theatre to improve their reputations. Even today, if you are doing a bunch of silly things on television, you occasionally go to work on the live stage to prove that you are indeed a serious actor.

So I sailed off to London and took on this challenge, but I had misgivings. I wondered if I would ever get to utter a word on the stage in London. I had no reputation whatsoever—but then I was offered a part as a lawyer in the London production of *Detective Story.* ⊡

Detective Story, *by Pulitzer Prize-winning American playwright Sidney Kingsley, ran on Broadway for 581 performances in 1949 and 1950. The British version at The Princes Theatre—now The Shaftesbury—opened in April 1950. The next year,* Detective Story *became a successful Hollywood film, directed by William Wyler.*

Austin Willis playing an American detective in Detective Story, *1950.*

Why would an unknown like me get this opportunity to act in what had the potential to be a stage hit? It dawned on me that Americans weren't easily allowed to work in England in the 1950s, but Canadians, as members of the British Commonwealth, could work without a permit. They were scouring the earth for actors to appear in this hit us play because they simply didn't have enough actors with credible American accents living in Great Britain.

They were paying me ten pounds a week to act in the play—a low salary, I thought. My apartment at Basil Street cost me ten pounds a week, so after I paid my rent, I couldn't afford to eat. I called up my BBC connections and learned that people in Boston and New York were complaining about British announcers on the imported newsreels shown in movie theatres before feature films. To Americans, it sounded like someone was talking with a mouthful of potatoes. The studio approached me to put my voice on Gaumont-British newsreels at ten pounds a week for six months. I was all set!

Accents are a funny thing, though. For an actor, they giveth and they taketh away. *Detective Story* was set in a police precinct in New York. The dear English audiences, who seemed to be able understand almost anyone from anywhere in the world, couldn't follow dialogue spoken by actors who were supposed to be from Brooklyn, the Bronx, or Manhattan. *Detective Story* closed in two weeks!

Friend or Foe

Back in Toronto, I was always interrupting my radio work for any opportunity to be onstage. I must have done fifteen to twenty plays directed by John Holden over the years. ⌑ Like a lot of people in Toronto at that time, I had a love/hate association with

John Porter Holden began a summer stock company, the Holden Players, in Bala, Ontario, in 1934. The company moved to Winnipeg, then Toronto, but faltered and eventually closed in 1941.

Nathan Cohen. He was the theatre critic for the *Toronto Star*, and he would come and see all our endeavours, wherever. Herbert Whittaker did theatre reviews for the *Globe and Mail* at that time, but Nathan was much harsher than Herbie. All of us looked somewhat askance at Nathan, but in other ways we loved him because he was a big, affable guy.

Nathan Cohen was originally from Cape Breton and was well-known for his acerbic, and even abrasive, style in print and on CBC Radio and Television from the 1940s through the 1960s. Herbert Whittaker was a Montreal-born stage designer and director who was drama critic at the Globe and Mail *from 1949 to 1975.*

I was doing a comedy a year, at least. Nathan would give me hideous reviews. He would say things like, "I went to see Austin Willis in a play last night at the Crest Theatre and I didn't laugh once. He was not funny at any time during the performance."

But I had performed that show to Nathan himself—because he was the best audience in the whole world. He was easy to spot because he had a preferred seat (stage left, or, if you were in the audience, the right-hand aisle). He booked the aisle seat because he had a bad leg. He would sit there, fourth row from the front, right in the stage lights. I played everything to Nathan because he never stopped laughing from the time I walked onto the stage until I left! Imagine my surprise the next day when I read what a terrible show I had done. Mind you, he occasionally gave me a very good review. But most were dreadful. And as I'll explain soon, one especially glowing review turned out to have a scorpion's sting.

My Best Friend Always

Back in Toronto I met and married Kate Reid—Canada's best actress ever. Kate had a special quality. It wasn't so much her acting—it was how she could make you *care* what happened to her characters that summoned the appreciation of her audience members. People cared so much about Kate that they fell into whatever she was projecting. She could have a walk-on as a maid, but she made audiences so interested in that maid that they wished she would come back instantly. She knew she had it, and she used it; she was so clever with it.

Even when Kate was badly cast, she would do extremely well. She was wonderful to play with, and we were together onstage many times. This country should be very proud of Kate Reid.

Kate Reid starred in over a thousand roles on stage, film, and television from the 1950s until her death in 1993. She played roles as varied as Aunt Lil Trotter on the TV series Dallas, *and Linda Loman in the TV movie of* Death of a Salesman. *She is often considered one of Canada's finest actresses.*

Very few people made the transition from radio to TV. All of us who had worked in radio drama or announcing or narrating—we were used to working with scripts in our hands. Learning lines was a laborious thing for me, and I had to work very hard at it. Along with her many other talents, Kate Reid was blessed with a photographic memory—learning lines was nothing to her. The only other person who was perhaps better was Orson Welles; he could just look at a page and commit it to memory with one reading.

Austin Willis had met Orson Welles when Welles came to Canada to participate in the Victory Loan *shows; he was also on set with him in Paris when they were shooting* Crack in the Mirror.

Kate wasn't quite that good, but she was close to it. Kate and I did quite a few shows together. The television show *Reunion* was a half-hour episode in a CBC Television series called *On Camera*. It was a "two-hander"—just Kate and I playing a separated couple. The scenario was that my character would be waiting for hers in a restaurant; she arrives and they play out a long scene together.

For two people to do an entire half-hour live show means that there are a lot of lines to learn. In this particular show, I wasn't at all confident just before the show started. I was sitting there practicing the lines with the producer when Kate went by and said, "You're still doing lines? My good heavens, I knew those lines a week ago."

I thought, *Yes, you devil, you did!* and she walked away.

It came time for the show to start; the dreaded red light came on and we got going. I was sitting at the table waiting for Kate. Finally, she came. I stood up, we said hello, and we sat down. I said something like, "Did you have any trouble finding the place?" but there was no answer. I asked again, and she had no answer for me. When someone "dries" and misses their lines, they get this peculiar look—shocked, or stunned, or dead. This was the way she looked. I knew that she had "gone up," as we say.

Poor Kate always had very tender feet, so I put my foot under the table and found one of her feet. I pressed it as hard as I could. I even half stood up. None of this was noticeable on camera. She came to and said, "What did you say?" I repeated my line and off we went. I was so pleased.

When the characters in *Reunion* leave, the situation that separated them is still there. It was a sad little piece, but interesting. I think we did it quite well. And again, it was live—with "live" the operative word here.

Career Versus Career

At the same time, our little family was growing. Our son Reid was four years old, Robin was a babe in arms, and we had a housekeeper. Then, a producer in London wanted both Kate and me, each for a different production. Kate was invited to do a play called *The Stepmother* with Judi Dench and Maggie Smith, and I was to play the American father of an American daughter (in an otherwise all-British cast) in *Roar Like a Dove*. In other words, I was going as a "second rater" in a comedy and wasn't expecting

Austin Willis married actress Kate Reid in 1954.

to do well. Kate was in a major production that was anticipated to make her a star. [co]

The Stepmother, *by Warren Chetham-Strode, is considered the only flop of Maggie Smith's career and was a serious blow to Kate Reid's.* Roar Like a Dove *was the premiere performance of a new comedy by the Scottish playwright Lesley Storm (the pen name of Mabel Cowie).*

Shortly after they approached me to go to London to do *Roar Like a Dove*, we got down to the nasty part—talking about the money. I asked, "Now, what kind of money are we talking about for me doing this?"

I was told that I was a "hundred pound boy." A hundred pounds a week was the top salary in the West End. Lawrence Olivier got paid a hundred pounds a week, too. But he, of course, owned some of each production he appeared in and earned a share of the profits. I calculated that £100 would be about $265 Canadian a week. I was probably smoking that much in those days!

As well, in theatre back then, you were required to supply your own costume. If you did a lot of work in England, this was a major consideration. If you had a big part in a play with four or

Austin Willis had top billing in Roar Like a Dove *in London, UK, 1957.*

five costume changes, you had to cart all that stuff with you and leave it at the theatre. The same applied to acting in movies in England. At one point, I had nothing left to wear at all, because all of my clothes were either at movie studios or at the theatre. Then, luckily, I put on weight and I had to buy a whole new set of clothes for the theatre—so I got my clothes back. Actors also had to supply a publicity shot for the front-of-house. In other words, to be an actor, you had to come totally equipped—all out of your own pocket.

Kate and I had a very tall, thin little house on Chester Row, just off Chester Square. It was a cute house, if a little weird. The kitchen was in the basement, and there was a dining room/sitting room on the next floor. At that time, author Mordecai Richler was living in London, too. He asked if he could come and talk to Kate and me.

I liked Mordecai very much; we used to take walks in Hyde Park together on nice afternoons and chat about Montreal. He was very curious about my family in Montreal and the Willis piano business. He knew more about my cousins than I did because he happened to circulate in that group of people. I never, at that time, realized his potential as a writer. I don't think anyone did; he was struggling to begin his career. He interviewed Kate and me for a magazine piece, of which I don't remember all that much, as lots of people were interviewing us for one thing and another.

Both Kate and I knew that she was the greater actress in our family. We adored each other. We had our two children, and it was a very happy time. What eventually felled our marriage was juggling the two careers. It

Mordecai Richler, who went on to fame as the author of The Apprenticeship of Duddy Kravitz, *was born in Montreal and had moved to London a few years before Austin Willis and Kate Reid, publishing seven of his ten novels and much of his journalism from London. Richler's gruff and opinionated views on most everything eventually became legendary.*

was not jealousy; we were okay until England. Then her play closed quickly and mine ran for a year. That made it very difficult. Kate was out of work and did maybe one television show in that time. She became very impatient, and when she got an offer from Stratford, she went home with the kids and I was left in London to complete my contract as well as some movies I had signed on to do.

Kate Reid moved to Stratford, Ontario, in 1959, after her stint in London, and she became central to the success of the Stratford Festival. She had great success playing Stratford's feisty ladies over the years. In 1962 she went on to play Martha in Who's Afraid of Virginia Woolf? *on Broadway, leading to twenty years of success on stage, film, and television in Canada and on Broadway.*

Having two careers on stage is very stressful for a marriage—but it has happened to hundreds and hundreds of people. In the end, we wound up unmarried—but still adoring one another. It was kind of sad because it was the business itself that did us in. Kate remained my dearest friend until the day she died, and she was good friends with Gwen, my present wife.

Kate Reid died in 1993 at the age of sixty-two, while living in Stratford.

The Scorpion's Sting

If you are in a play that runs for a year, you get to know a lot of lovely people in the cast. It becomes a great big family—and you're closer to them than you are to your real family by the end, because you're with them every day. The first thing you do when you come in for your performance is to check in with everyone—how was your day, what did you do, etc.

It was getting on in the year's run of *Roar Like a Dove*—around the end of August, I think. I came to the Phoenix Theatre one night and went downstairs to ask how everyone was doing. Nobody spoke to me. Next, I checked in with the lead, Pat Barr, in the big dressing room downstairs. He just turned his back to me and walked away. ▣

I went to Margalo Gillmore, a famous actress from New York

Patrick Barr was a popular British actor from the 1930s to the 1980s, invariably playing authority figures and reliable friends.

who was playing my wife; I tried to give her a hug and she turned away from me! I was bewildered. What had I done to make my friends turn on me? I put my tail between my legs and decided to disappear into my dressing room. Then someone advised me to go and read the notice board. I ran downstairs and on the board there was a clipping from the *Toronto Star*—a column by Nathan Cohen. It was a glowing report about how I was really showing the British how to do drawing-room comedy. As you can imagine, those words stung the rest of the cast and caused them to give me the cold shoulder. It took me a long time to repair that damage. I don't think I ever forgave Nathan for that review—and it was a positive one!

Hazards of Success

One of the side problems to a long run is that, because you see quite a lot of the people you're working with, you can sometimes get on each other's nerves. To solve this we had what we called a Bore Bottle—an empty whisky bottle. If anyone came in during the evening and took too long recounting his day's activities, or told a story everyone had heard before, or was too pompous about any facet of his life—then someone would go get the "Bore Bottle" and hand it to the culprit, who would have to pay a six-pence fine.

I went a bit squirrelly with the success of this play. About eight months into *Roar Like a Dove*, I was doing a two-handed scene during a matinee. I was sitting on a sofa while the other actor was in the back making drinks. He had a long monologue, and then I was supposed to launch into a huge speech. He delivered his bit and finished with my cue line: "Isn't that right, Tom?"

He got no answer. He tried again, and still received no answer from me, so he came over, handed me my drink, and gave me a little whack on the side of my face. I took the drink but didn't say a word. Slowly the curtain came down and everyone rushed over to me, asking what was the matter. Because we were eight months into the play, my mind had drifted off in the middle of the performance; I was wondering if I might have to file my income tax in both Toronto and England.

I had "dried." It was a terrible experience. I shook for a couple of days and totally lost my confidence, which is a terrible thing for an actor. That's what a long run did to me; I had never done a run that long. The Brits were used to being in such box office hits, and the same for New York actors—but this was unheard of for an actor from the Canadian stage. I never got used to it.

Holding it Together

Still, I had great adventures and a lot of fun in London. I have to tell you about my dresser, Charlie Crimp.⊡ Charlie dressed me in *Roar Like a Dove* and went on movie shoots with me, and was probably with me for about four years. He was an excellent dresser, but the cast told me up front that Charlie was very sensitive—mainly about the hideous, ratty-looking toupée that he wore. I was told to never let on that I suspected he was wearing one.

A dresser is an assistant who handles a performer's costumes.

Charlie kept this "rug" on his head with a piece of black electrical tape. Part of his job as the dresser was to put on my shoes. I hated this; I can put on my own shoes, and I thought it must feel most demeaning to be slipping someone else's feet into their shoes. But Charlie insisted that I let him do his duty. To make things even more awkward, every time he bent down to put on my shoes, the "rug" would start to slide off. I would gently put my hand on it and hold it in place. Charlie never let on, and neither did I. We performed this pantomime eight times a week, and I never told anybody our secret.

Occasionally, during the run of a play, I would be shooting scenes for a movie at a studio in the daytime. Charlie went on location for a lot of pictures with me, and one morning I had to wake up about 4:30. Charlie would always say, "Here, guv; have this cup of coffee, guv," and I would take a sip. On this particular morning, it was straight brandy. I was drunk for the first two hours of the day.

One performance during the run was particularly special. In a play like *Roar Like a Dove*, you would start off the week with a batch of clean shirts for all the changes you had, and then on Thursday night, they would give you new shirts. One week we had new shirts by Tuesday night, and I asked what was going on. Charlie explained that the Queen would be in that night.

We gave a bully show. Everyone was marvellous. We finished, and I went upstairs to my dressing room, which comprised a small sitting room and a little room behind it, where I took my clothes off. Charlie was helping me change into my "go-home" pants and "go-home" shirt when there was a knock on the door. Charlie went to answer it and came back to say, "Guv—there's a lady out there to see you. She says she's the Queen."

There, sure enough, standing in the hallway, was Queen Elizabeth II. I didn't know whether to curtsy or bow. I blurted out, "I'm sorry to keep you waiting, Ma'am. Sir."

"That's quite all right," she said. "I did enjoy your performance. I'm coming back again. You were wonderful." She added, "You're Canadian—how nice," and off she went down the hall.

SEVEN

Stage and Screen—
Away from North America

At the same time that I was doing *Roar Like a Dove* at the Phoenix Theatre I was shooting a film called *The Mouse That Roared*. 🎞

As had been the case when I'd performed on the stage in *Detective Story* the filmmakers needed someone who could look and sound like a convincing American, and Canadians were "legal" in Britain in these days—we could work with a permit, unlike actors from the States. I played the American Secretary of Defense who negotiated with the mythical and miniscule Duchy of Grand Fenwick.

The Mouse That Roared was a British film satirizing the Cold War and starring Peter Sellers; it had a modest budget and modest ambitions but became a surprise hit in America. Its premise was that, if the tiny European Duchy of Grand Fenwick invaded the States, it would be defeated and then be eligible for the kind of aid the US gave to its vanquished Second World War enemies—but through an improbable series of coincidences, it defeated America and then dictated the terms of peace.

While playing three roles in *The Mouse That Roared*, Peter Sellers was in the same tricky situation that I was—he was also in a play in the West End. He came up to me one day on the movie set and made the most amazing proposal to me.

He asked, "Are you tired?"

"Yes," I replied, "*very*, because I am doing the play and then getting up at this unreasonable hour in the morning to get here."

"I have an idea," he said. "Let's you and I hire an ambulance! It sleeps two. We can have them pick us up at the theatres and then we can drive down here and park outside the makeup room and gain two or three hours' sleep."

I said, "That's a great idea—I'll go half with you."

So an ambulance turned up the next night. Much to the amazement of my cast, I put on my pajamas and dressing gown after my performance. I collected quite a little crowd at the stage door as we drove off to Shepperton Studios, miles and miles outside London.

The only problem was that Sellers brought a bottle of Scotch with him. In fact, we both brought bottles and had a great party—and got less sleep than before. By the time we got outside the makeup room at Shepperton we were both pretty merry—and woke up the next morning feeling like death. It turned out that it wasn't actually a good idea, so we gave up the ambulance.

Peter Sellers had recently bought a new Rolls Royce and was fascinated with all of its knobs and buttons. It was the first car I'd seen with a telephone. Of course, we all had to go out and sit in it while he telephoned people all over the world. One day I was sitting with him in the car, waiting to do an outdoor scene, and it was raining out. An assistant came over and asked us to do the scene. I put my hand out and reminded him that it was still raining. He said, "Yes, Mr. Willis, in England if we had to wait for it to stop raining to make a movie, we never would make one—so come along."

Sellers and I travelled around England together doing promotion for *The Mouse That Roared*. We would appear sometimes at movie theatres before the show and talk to the audience. Peter Sellers was a wonderful actor and great fun to be with—but he also had mood swings like many funny men do, it seems.

I truly enjoyed making that picture, but I never had the opportunity to work with him again.

The War That Never Ended

While I was based in England I also did a film in Germany—*I Aim at the Stars*, a biographical film about the German rocket scientist Wernher von Braun, who had developed the v-2 rocket for the Nazis and had surrendered to Allied troops near the end of the Second World War. I played another American, this time General John Medaris, who had brought von Braun into the us rocket development program.

I made a great friend of Jurgens, who played von Braun, and spent a weekend at his forest lodge, where we talked about our careers. He had been the captain of a u-boat in the German navy. We figured out that one night, when I was with the Canadian torpedo boat flotilla and he was with his u-boat, we might have passed in the English Channel and may even have fired at one another.

I accidentally cost this production a lot of money one day by having my wristwatch set at the wrong time when I pointed to a clock on the wall. My watch contradicted the time on the clock—which was essential to the storyline. We had to reshoot this scene, and I have never forgotten the embarrassment that I caused this film.

But there were worse problems. When we were filming at the legendary Babelsberg studios outside Berlin, the filmmakers were

> *I Aim at the Stars, starring Curt Jurgens and directed by J. Lee Thompson, was released in 1960.*

unknowingly using an old ammunition dump to film the picture's rocket tests. When the explosives from our movie went off, they ignited explosives underground, and everything blew up. Huge oak trees flew into the air. I hid behind the biggest tree that I could find. Two fellows were killed and several were injured. It was a staggeringly awful thing to happen.

Austin Willis sported a moustache for I Aim at the Stars, *1960.*

Cigars, Noses, and Love

The other picture I did while I was living in London was *Crack in the Mirror*, which was shot in Paris. Orson Welles stayed at the George v, a beautiful hotel in Paris. I stayed at hotel called the San Francisco because I could pronounce it. The movie's drivers picked me up last each morning, and by that time I couldn't see who else was in the car because of Orson's cigar smoke. He lit one up first thing in the morning. By the time we got to the studio, maybe six o'clock in the morning, I was sick to my stomach. But he was merry, talking away— and puffing away.

Crack in the Mirror *was a 1960 drama directed by Richard Fleischer and starring Orson Welles, Juliette Gréco, and Bradford Dillman. The producer was Darryl Zanuck. Fleischer later gave Austin Willis one of his best roles, as the doctor in* The Boston Strangler.

Orson Welles always had a prosthetic nose, and he never made a movie except *The Third Man* with his own nose. He must have hated his own nose. He held up shooting *Crack in the Mirror* for two weeks until his nose arrived from New York. When it did arrive, the difference was indiscernible to me, but never mind. Orson put it on and everyone had to remark on what a marvellous nose it was.

Orson ran everything. He wasn't the director, but he directed the picture. Orson was a pleasure to work with, though, because there was never a dull second.

One day Brother Frank intervened in the midst of all this. He was hosting *the* CBC Television public affairs program of the day, *Close-Up,* and his producer called, asking me do an interview with Zanuck and Juliette Gréco, who was Zanuck's girlfriend at the time. Essentially, this picture was being made for her.

I got the feeling the CBC wanted me to make the interview controversial. They sent a French-Canadian (Radio-Canada) CBC crew from Paris. I do not speak a word of French, but somehow I had to interpret what my two interview subjects were saying to the French crew.

We set up for the interview and my first question for Zanuck and Gréco was, "When do you two plan to get married?"

They both got up and stormed out. I figured that I was going to get the pink slip the next day, but they came back and we had a laugh about it, and then I did a patsy of an interview and sent it to Toronto.

I got one word back from Brother Frank: "Love!"

Cancellation

My last play in London started promisingly but turned into a slowly unfolding tragedy. It was a thing called *Man and Boy* with Charles Boyer.⏍ It was written by a great British comedic writer called Terence Rattigan, and we had high hopes for it. We opened at the Theatre Royal in Brighton, the popular seaside destination outside London. It had a terrific advance audience because of Charles Boyer, and our first show was filled with people looking to buy the rights for further runs, and potentially for a film. I had second billing, so at the end of the first performance we took a curtain call together. As we bowed, Charles took my hand, and when we went down, he said to me very clearly: "'Tis a dog."

Charles Boyer was a suave French actor and Hollywood matinee idol throughout the 1930s and '40s. Boyer plied his considerable charm on live theatre stages in the latter part of his career, particularly in The Marriage-Go-Round, *from 1958 to 1960.*

Unfortunately, we were scheduled in London for fourteen weeks and in New York for as long as it would run.

There were seven people in the play. In my lifetime, five of them would go on to commit suicide, including Charles Boyer. That was awfully hard to live with. When Charles killed himself in 1976, my fellow survivor from the original cast, Geoffrey Keen, called me in London. At the end of a sombre conversation, dear Geoffrey said, "Boy—you don't suppose it was us, do you?"

EIGHT

Making It in America— or Trying to

an and Boy made it to New York, and while I was
there, Sammy Davis Jr. asked me to play his manager in his upcoming revision of *Golden Boy.* ⊡ We
were long-time friends, and he just needed me to
audition—but I had to sing! Never ask an actor if he can do anything, because he will always say, "Yes, of course!"

I immediately panicked. I
got hold of my agent and asked
him to find somebody to play
the piano for me. I went to the
pianist's studio religiously and
worked with him every day. I
thought he was a very grumpy
old man because he was never very enthusiastic about my singing—what a grouch!

> *The 1964 musical adaptation of the*
> *1938 original of* Golden Boy *for the*
> *multi-talented Davis ran for more*
> *than five hundred performances.*
> *Sammy Davis Jr. was a leading force*
> *in American popular music and*
> *culture before the "British Invasion"*
> *in 1964.*

Maybe he was trying to tell me something.

I prepared two tunes: "September Song" and the very popular "Try To Remember" from the musical comedy *The Fantasticks*. [ ] I wouldn't have to do anything else but sing, because they already knew I could act.

"September Song" was an American pop standard composed by Kurt Weill, with lyrics by Maxwell Anderson, first introduced on Broadway in 1938.

I walked into the Helen Hayes Theatre for my audition. The set was illuminated by a single bare light bulb. From where I was standing, I couldn't see who was in the audience. I sang "September Song"—or at least I got about a verse and half of "September Song" out—when into the light walked a familiar fellow covered from head to foot in bracelets and chains. Sammy Davis Jr. waved his hand and said, "That's enough! That's fine, Mr. Willis." When he got closer, he said, "Austin, you're a very fine actor. But you've got some nerve trying to sing."

The penny dropped as to why my piano player had been less than enthusiastic.

I exited gracefully from that stage and remained friends with Sammy Davis Jr. for the rest of my life.

Goldfinger and my Golden Wrist

Many of the films I made in those years were never shown in America, but the blockbuster *Goldfinger*, paradoxically, may have been my greatest lost opportunity. [ ] My agent offered me a part in this picture because our play *Man and Boy* had bombed so spectacularly, and I had some time on my hands. I could either play the American Secret Service agent who briefs his friend Bond—or I could smile and play Simmons, who plays gin rummy with Auric

Goldfinger was the third film in the James Bond series starring Sean Connery; it recouped its production costs within two weeks of opening.

Goldfinger. I chose the more substantial card-playing role and, given the movie's success, the role did indeed yield lovely royalties over the years.

But none of us could foresee the longevity of the James Bond franchise, and playing the American CIA agent would have been a lovely sustaining gig. During the filming, the character I played was in a car chase, a fist fight, and had lunch in a diner with Bond and Goldfinger.

I have never since been on a set or a stage where we spent so much time just waiting. On four successive mornings, I was called to the makeup room at the studio at 7:00 A.M., but I was not called to actually work before the cameras until 3:30 on the afternoon of the fourth day. By that time, I didn't care if I worked at all. I'd written letters to everybody that I knew in England,

Austin Willis winning at gin rummy in Goldfinger, *1964.*

Canada, and the United States. I had read two books. I had filed my fingernails down to one inch below the quick!

Goldfinger was certainly the largest-budget film that I was ever involved with—and I inadvertently, again, added to those costs, as I had with *I Aim at the Stars*. We shot the scene in which I was playing cards at the Hotel Fontainebleau in Miami Beach, but no one saw the rushes until they got back to England, where most of the film was being shot. When they zoomed in on my hand of cards, I was wearing a bracelet that clearly identified me as "Austin Willis"—and you could not miss it. They had to rebuild the set in England to reshoot that scene. I can't imagine what that must have cost them.

My card game in *Goldfinger* turned out to be the shortest part in the longest movie I was ever on. I worked for eight weeks and I was in about six quite long scenes—all of which ended up on the cutting room floor.

One Christmas in Toronto, I took my family to see *Goldfinger* at the Odeon Theater at the corner of College and Yonge Streets. It was a very snowy night, so we were running late. My kids were not very old, and I got us seats in the front row of the balcony so they'd have a good view—but by the time we got seated up there, the card scene with Goldfinger was over.

All through the picture my dear daughter Robin kept saying, "When are you going to be on, Daddy?"

Of course, I wasn't. As the evening went on, I felt smaller and smaller.

When in Rome, Hold Your Horses

While I was living in London, I also had the dubious distinction of being in the most expensive pilot that did not make it as a television series. *The Barbarians* was shot by Paramount Studios in Rome for prime time Sunday nights on NBC in 1960. We worked on it for fourteen weeks, with the script being changed almost daily. I was a disgraced old Roman centurion who had been pitched out of the government, and I was trying to help the slaves gain ground and find some kind of a life that didn't involve torture. Jack Palance was a "Barbarian" who helped lead the slaves in their struggle for freedom, and we were working together. ⊡ My charac-

ter could advise his because I was wise and knew Rome from top to bottom, because I had been high up in the government until I was thrown out.

> *Jack Palance was a professional boxer in the 1930s who went on to have a notable stage and film career in the 1940s and '50s.*

Unfortunately I wound up in the hospital two or three times because Jack Palance wouldn't go to sword school. Sword fighting is like a ballet: you learn to do it by numbers so the other guy knows what you are doing. We were fighting on the same side and stood back-to-back a lot, fending off attackers on the deck of a ship. Every time Jack pulled his sword back, he would hit me on the top of my head, so I bled a lot.

My other job in *The Barbarians*, besides sword fighting, was that I had to drive a chariot. I had to practice driving one with four horses, and I could never figure out the business of winding the reins around your wrist. Whenever I had spare time, they would bring the horses around and I would practice. There was a little track right inside the studio we were using, and I would trot these horses around this track to see if the horses would pay any attention. Of course, they didn't!

Then Palance would come and stand on the chariot so the horses would get used to us, since we rode together in most of our scenes. One day as we were doing this, for reasons unknown to me, the horses decided to go home—back to the barn, which was not located at the studio. Outside the studio there was a four-lane superhighway (equivalent to Toronto's 401). My not-so-trusty steeds ran onto this freeway. Not only that—they were going in the wrong direction! Tires were squealing and Italian drivers were cursing. The horses only had to travel about fifty metres to get home, and they knew exactly where they were headed, so they got us off the highway safely. It took me three weeks to get over that.

My only consolation on that film was that I was wearing a toga with leather thongs on my arms, and I looked great. I was in good shape in those days, because I smoked a lot—maybe 150 cigarettes a day—which is why I can't breathe today. (Cigarettes are very hard to hide in a toga, so I stashed mine in a pouch tied around my waist.)

We also wore a lot of body paint underneath our togas and I remember being directed to a line of marble showers after our first day of shooting. Each shower had a woman in it. The women were supposed to wash us down—but this Nova Scotian wasn't going to have anybody wash him! I took a cab back to the Residence Palace Hotel where we were staying and showered there.

The Barbarians was expected to take *Bonanza*'s place in the Sunday night schedule, but its ratings were bad as soon as it started. *Bonanza* had been expensive to make, so they'd pulled the trigger on it after airing just four of the eight episodes that had been made—but then they put the other four episodes on air just to fill time, and *Bonanza* turned into a hit. We were sitting around after filming the orgy scene (where the worst thing we did was eat grapes), and I remember hearing that we were cancelled. To save their investment, they edited the series into a movie and released it. I have never seen the thing.

NINE

Back to Canada

While I was shooting these movies in Europe I was keeping my hand in with the CBC back home. I couldn't pass up any offers, and in one year I flew across the Atlantic seven or eight times, trying to keep my hand in in both worlds. The airfare exceeded what people were paying me, so despite all the work it wasn't a good summer financially. I didn't know where I wanted to be. I wanted so much to work from England, but the money just didn't work out.

You dressed up to fly in those days. I always took care with how I looked and what I was wearing—and I enjoyed that. I still have some of my favourite suits from those days—though I don't get much of a chance to wear them anymore. I lost the necklace of sharks' teeth that was perfectly fashionable in my time—I but did bring some of my favourite hats with me to Dartmouth.

I remember one suit in particular, as I was wearing it on a disastrous trip overseas from Montreal. I was quite pleased with this suit, but when I got up to go to the washroom I felt something on my backside: air. My pants had ripped open at the seam, from the fly right up the back to my belt, so I had two legs that were not joined. That was all very well as long as I could sit in my seat and be hidden, but we were close to making our landing, and I had to get up and get off the plane. The flight attendant was very nice to me, but it was the most hideous trip from the plane to get a taxi to greater London—because all the while, I was awkwardly trying to hide my white underwear shorts.

Austin wearing his "fashionable" shark-tooth necklace.

Warden of the Plains

In the early 1960s we had a great hit with the play *Once More With Feeling*, directed by my old friend John Holden, at the Manitoba Theatre Centre. ⊡ They doubled the run from four weeks to eight while we were still in rehearsal—unusual for a Canadian stage production.

Once More with Feeling, *by Harry Kurnitz, opened to a long run on Broadway in 1958 and later became a successful British comedy film starring Yul Brynner.*

The play's success became a really big deal—and not just in Winnipeg. I was given the keys to several Manitoba communities, made an honorary "Warden of the Plains," and appointed honorary chief of a dozen Indigenous communities. To top it off, an Austin Willis Day was declared in Moose Jaw and they actually had a parade for me!

On the day of the parade, the women who worked at the Birks jewellery store were watching from the slanted shelf by the window where they displayed their wares. Just as we were passing, the shelf gave out, and one of the ladies fell forward with it, through the glass. The whole parade stopped to make sure she was okay. Luckily, she was.

I used to brag about how *Once More With Feeling* allowed me to set a record for attendance at each performance, and for attendance over the length of the run at the Manitoba Theatre Centre. But guess who broke my record? None other than Kate Reid, when they brought *Who's Afraid of Virginia Woolf?* to Winnipeg.

Perhaps the best result of my becoming "Warden of the Plains" was that it annoyed my bother Frank—who, like most Maritimers, is really a cowboy at heart.

The theatre folks in Winnipeg had heard about our success with *Roar Like a Dove* in London; they liked me so much they asked

Austin Willis in Once More With Feeling *at the Manitoba Theatre Centre, 1962.*

me to direct and star in the play for them. As always, I was game. I was thrilled to try my hand as a director. Unfortunately, I failed as miserably as I had as a singer! I could act. I could show them how to act. But I couldn't direct—and I never directed again.

A Canadian Cowboy Flick

While I was in demand, I was enticed to make another Canadian film—a Western on the plains of Owen Sound. I was the sheriff and the villain in *Wolf Dog*, with second billing to Jim Davis.

Jim Davis was an American actor who played primarily in Westerns; he eventually became Jock Ewing on Dallas. Wolf Dog *was never considered a commercial or artistic success—though it is still beloved in Markdale, Ontario, where it can be viewed at the local library.*

Here come the horses again. I spent all my time in this film on horseback, and that gave me a lifelong hatred of horses—not the dear animals themselves, but having to ride them. My horses always "went back to the barn," no matter what I tried to do with them. The crew went so far as to give me a pair of spurs to wear, but that just meant that the horse would run back to the barn even faster.

With *Wolf Dog* we didn't have trained movie horses, just local horses rented for the occasion. When you make movies, the crew sets marks (crosses made of chalk or wood) that indicate where you are to deliver particular scenes. That is where the camera expects you to be when you are delivering your lines. Trained horses in Hollywood would hit the marks themselves. With *Wolf Dog*, I was the sheriff leading this huge posse of maybe twenty guys. Every time they set up for a shot, someone would be holding my horse's halter. Then they would run away and the scene would start. As soon as they left, the horse would turn and head for the barn. Everyone was hysterical because I was supposed to be their fearless leader.

To make matters worse, one of my best friends, John Hart, was in *Wolf Dog*. ⊡ John had that distinctive "Western" look and could ride a horse wonderfully. We had a scene that involved a horse chase, and we had this beautiful palomino with a white tail and white mane. John had to ride the horse across a field at a dead run.

John Hart was a Hollywood actor who appeared in many Westerns and was best known for playing the Lone Ranger for a single season in 1954.

The cameraman got what he needed on the first take, and John walked the horse back while everyone waited so we could shoot the next scene. I asked him why the devil he walked the horse back and he said, "Aust, I was only paid to go one way. There's so many holes in that field, I was lucky to do it."

I couldn't relax with horses, so I went to a stable in Kleinburg, Ontario, to learn to ride. And who should come riding through the woods, very comfortable on his horse, but my old friend from CBC Radio, Lorne Greene.

"What are you doing here?" I demanded. "I've got an excuse."

Lorne said, "So have I—I'm

Bonanza debuted on NBC in 1959, running through to 1973 with Lorne Greene playing Ben Cartwright, the patriarch, in every episode.

going to do a pilot for a series in Hollywood." That series was *Bonanza*. ⊡

Playing Hockey on Film

We were always trying to make the definitive hockey film in Canada, and I had my own go at it a couple of times. I played an aging hockey player in an early CBC Television drama called *Ice on Fire*. Then, I played the legendary owner of the Toronto Maple Leafs in *Face-Off*, a feature film in which we had some NHL hockey players playing themselves. We had tried unsuccessfully to make many hockey pictures in the old days, but they hadn't worked, because it was a hard game to photograph. The real game of hockey was always a lot better than anything we could dramatize. George McCowan was a splendid director, and he did a wonderful job of filming the players on roller skates because so many of the actors couldn't skate on ice. ▢

Austin Willis as a hockey magnate in Face-Off, *1971.*

True Confessions

Many of us drank more than we should have in the 1950s and '60s—particularly after our performances. One American woman, a very skilled actress (whose name I am not going to divulge), took this even further: she was inclined to have a tipple *before* she performed each night. John Holden insisted on her doing the play because he had seen her do it somewhere and had been impressed. John thought her tippling did not interfere with her performance, though I felt it sometimes did. She has long since gone to heaven—or at least I prefer to believe that's the direction she took—but as the run extended, I never knew what state she would be in when I walked on stage. The cast privately referred to her as "Miss Vodka of 1953."

Here's another confession from my time in the theatre, because that's where I felt most at home: I am not good at remembering names. I can be introduced to someone, and thirty seconds later I can't recall that person's name. Maybe I don't pay attention? It's something I'm rather ashamed of.

This trait seems common among actors the world over. We are notoriously bad at remembering people's names. I am told this is because, in any city, no matter how big it is, there is a community of actors. These people all know each other very well, and a great number of them socialize together most of the time—when they are not working and even when they are working. They get in a play with one another, though, and suddenly they need to use the character's name all the time. In real life, they might be Don or Diane or Lesley, but in the play, they could be Claude or Louise or Christie. And unlike their real names, those character names are repeated every night for weeks. So in real life when an acting friend turns up, I don't bother worrying myself—I just call him or her "dear," which works fine. I am told this is why you hear so much "dear" and "darling" in the conversations of theatre people.

Vaudeville in Kleinburg

In the early 1960s I was back at the studios in Kleinburg, Ontario, making a very interesting and memorable film called *Ten Girls Ago*, which you will not have heard of. The filmmakers brought together Bert Lahr, Eddie Foy Jr., and Buster Keaton to make a

Austin Willis in Ten Girls Ago, *shot in 1962 and never completed.*

vaudeville-style comedy that was intended to be a breakout film for the singing sensation Dion. I was completely in awe of all these comic legends and was supposed to keep them in line as the "TV news director"—although I do remember swinging from a chandelier in one shot.

Dion DiMucci was an American pop singer who climbed to stardom in the late 1950s with Dion and the Belmonts. Buster Keaton was a fading vaudevillian best known for his silent films and deadpan physical comedy. Eddie Foy Jr. was an American actor and scion of the famous vaudeville family that had been immortalized in the 1955 Hollywood film The Seven Little Foys. *Bert Lahr had played the cowardly lion in the legendary* Wizard of Oz *and was now nearing the end of his career.*

These three legendary comics were always nervous about the financial side of every job—and this film was no different. To watch those three faces worrying was a very depressing sight.

Unfortunately, our paycheques from the first week of work came back with a cheery little message: "Try again."

You can imagine their reactions! They instantly retired to their dressing rooms and refused to budge until this "try again" situation was cleared up—which it soon was. New cheques were issued, which we promptly presented to the local bank in the town of Kleinburg (which at that time was situated in a trailer, as the bank was under construction).

Now, with our money assured, we returned to work and everything went swimmingly until the following week, when our paycheques were distributed promptly—but this time there was a note attached from the producers cheerily asking us to "please cash this as soon as possible so we'll know where we are."

Well, Bert Lahr, the most nervous of the whole group, started out the door, running to the bank, which was two miles away, without even waiting for the car we all piled into. We finally managed to catch up with him. Our cheques cleared with no more problems—but then a flood of technical mishaps caused the

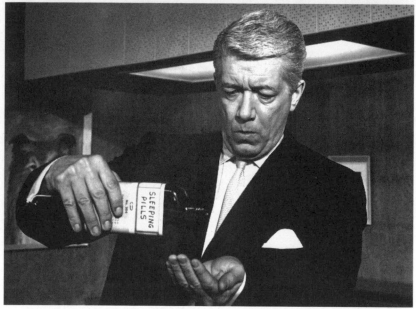

TOP AND BOTTOM: *Austin Willis as a confused television director in* Ten Girls Ago, *1962.*

producers to try to wrap the film up quickly, which destroyed any storyline that they have may have started with. The film was

> *Thirty-two minutes of footage from Ten Girls Ago survives and is housed at the National Archives of Canada.*

never completed—but it had been a memorable time for me.◫

Enemies, Neighbours, and Founding Fathers

I greatly enjoyed doing a CBC Television drama called *Who Needs an Enemy?* I was pleased with my work in it. It was a story about a business, and about people in business. The fellow I played was rather a rotter, insofar as he had no compunction about cheating and doing evil things, trying to get the best of his colleagues. I had a big part in it, and it was a very difficult part to play. When you are playing something that is really quite villainous, it is hard to be the leading man and keep the attention of the audience— without them hating you outright.

But my character was also a pleasant rake, in a way. He loved the ladies but didn't want to marry. Anna Cameron played a woman who tricked him into getting married, and his reaction to

> *Anna Cameron was a Toronto actress (and the best friend of Kate Reid) who moved to Halifax in the 1980s.*

that was quite difficult to do.◫ I thought it was a skillful piece in that way, and I loved the cast we had.

Also, I'm very proud of *Neighbours* and am proud that the CBC took it on. It was a difficult story about a Black couple who move into a white neighbourhood, and it was a courageous story to do back in 1964.◫

I also got to play a founding father of Canada: Alexander Galt. It was 1964 and a bunch of

> Neighbours: A Play *was written by Arkady Leokum and dramatized for the* CBC *Television series* Show of the Week. *It was directed by Paul Almond. Ruby Dee and Ossie Davis were brought to Toronto to perform with Austin Willis and Corrine Conley.*

actors were enlisted to re-enact the 1864 trip taken by the Fathers of Confederation from Quebec City to Charlottetown. We did everything that they had done. We went to Quebec City and stayed overnight at the Château Frontenac. Then we got on a boat. The producers had taken an old cable ship and put a phony bow on it to look like the *Queen Victoria*, the official Government of Canada steamship. We sailed to Prince Edward Island with all the same stops, and did all the things they had done (as far as could be discerned from the archives). We were also bused to places like Moncton and Fredericton. We were being filmed constantly—but I have no idea whether this ever made it to television or not.

Diversifying

To make a living in those days you had to do it all. If you were just an actor you couldn't make much of a living. You had to host TV and radio shows, do commercials, plus be an actor—whatever was available. You were working pretty hard. My schedule included a daily radio program of an hour and a half—and three television shows a week. Then I might pick up a few extra dollars by providing the back of my head—as extras had done on *Cross-Canada Hit Parade*—where heads were needed for background.

I was also the spokesman for Firestone Tires, and one night I had to go from being the prosecuting attorney in a courtroom drama called *Collision* to doing a live commercial about tires. The drama was about a collision at sea, and I was not getting a cue from anybody as I started questioning my witnesses. Bruno Gerussi was one of them, and when I forgot my opening line I asked him who he was, hoping he would help me get back on track. Bruno started to giggle, prompting me to giggle.

Bruno Gerussi was an actor from Medicine Hat, Alberta, who became best known for his role as Nick Adonidas in CBC's longest-running dramatic series, The Beachcombers, *in the 1970s and 1980s.*

Luckily, we had to go to commercial break. I had to rush into the other studio and do a one-minute commercial with no teleprompter, no anything. So there I was, sitting at a desk with a Firestone tire in a cardboard stand. As I got into the commercial, I started to remember my lines from *Collision* and feel more confident. I ended the commercial by banging on the tire to emphasize that *this was the tire was for anybody and everybody*. The tire promptly jumped out of its cardboard stand and rolled off the desk and out of the studio. I got up and followed the tire.

When I got home that evening the telephone rang. Guess who? Yes, it was Brother Frank. He said, "I thought you were very good tonight in the drama, but I have a question about the commercial. When the tire jumped out of its holder and you didn't need it anymore—why did you follow it?"

The Esso Man

Speaking of commercials, I have to tell you the story of my great friend, Murray Westgate—perhaps the most successful actor in Canada—who did commercials as an Esso service man during CBC's NHL hockey broadcasts. We had first met when we were sailing from St. John's, Newfoundland, for Londonderry in Northern Ireland on a naval corvette, where Murray was the navigating officer. He was very interested in what I was doing because I had a tape recorder, and I was recording interviews with members of the crew to send back home. He asked me how I got into the business (and how he could), and the best advice I could give him was to bang on a lot of doors. We had no schools.

Murray made a great success of being *the* Esso Man in the 1950s and 1960s. But when he finished with Esso, nobody

Austin Willis's colleague and friend Lorne Greene offered Canada's first broadcasting training at his Lorne Greene School of Broadcasting in Toronto after the Second World War.

would hire him as an actor—no one could imagine him as anyone but the friendly service-station character. It took Murray a long time to get his other leg down and get in the business again. As the years went by and we all got older and retired, Murray was also coming to the end of his career—although he had not been doing very much. Esso decided they were going to remake the commercial about the Esso Man, because they had a younger Esso Man now. They arranged this commercial and contacted Murray's agent, who told them that if they wanted Murray Westgate, they were going to have to pay an outrageous price. The negotiator at the other end was outraged and nearly fainted. But they paid Murray what was asked, so this story had a happy ending. ▢

Murray Westgate was nominated for a Genie award in 1988 for his role in the feature film Blue City Slammers, *and in 1991 he played the Esso Service Man one more time. Westgate died in August 2018, after celebrating his one hundredth birthday in the spring of that year.*

Murray also developed hobbies as we all did when we were not working. In Murray's case he became an accomplished visual artist—and I am so pleased that his caricature of me appears in the pages of this book.

Commanding the Seaway

Seaway, a 1965 CBC Television dramatic series about investigating crime in the shipping industry, was a very promising project. The scripts were very good, and excellent actors were brought in from California. It was shot on location on ships on the St. Lawrence River, with helicopters and all the gear we could muster.

I was playing Admiral Fox—"Foxy" to his colleagues—in charge of the police force protecting the Canada/US border, with Stephen Young and Cec Linder as my co-stars. We had British funding so the show was being seen in Great Britain; we were also expecting it to go into American distribution. We made thirty

Actor Murray Westgate, best known as the Esso Man, was also a talented
caricaturist, and he created this caricature of Austin Willis.

episodes and were on the verge of negotiating American distribution—when American television switched to broadcasting in colour. The show was the most expensive series ever shot in Canada in black and white, but our British investors could not afford to convert the production to colour. *Seaway* was cancelled after the first season, and I was most disappointed.

Seaway *was a Canadian-British television co-production created by Abraham Polonsky. With a budget of $3 million, it was the most ambitious dramatic series created in Canada, costing $100,000 per episode. The show featured well-known and highly respected actors such as Barry Morse, Gordon Pinsent, Sally Kellerman, Faye Dunaway, and Richard Thomas.*

Austin Willis commanding the set of Seaway, *1966–1967.*

Austin Willis was a little nervous shooting this helicopter scene in Seaway, *1966–1967.*

TEN

Go Big—or Stay Home

I decided to go to Hollywood. *Seaway* had been cancelled and I was at a loss as to what to do next. I thought, "Everyone is sick of me in Canada now, so I'll go off to Hollywood."

I moved into the Chateau Marmont on Sunset Boulevard, where anybody visiting from Europe would be staying. [m]

This was a weird hotel. I did not know what to make of it. There was no dining room, no room service. It was Moorish-looking, Spanish-looking. But it was very comfortable. Since they allowed pets, I went there with Foxy, the little Yorkshire terrier I got when I finished the series *Seaway*.

Beatrice Lillie was also staying at the Chateau Marmont, and she had her very famous cocker spaniel, Lord Buttons, with her. [co]

The Chateau Marmont was built in 1929 in Los Angeles and has always been the iconic "Old World" Hollywood place of accommodation.

Beatrice Lillie was a Canadian-born British actress, singer, and performer who was active from 1914 to 1966. In 1953, she won a Tony Award for her Broadway revue, An Evening with Beatrice Lillie.

Lord Buttons and Foxy became very friendly during their walks every evening; they trotted along together and everything was great. I wrote Brother Frank right away.

"You will be glad to know that I am very comfortable at the Chateau Marmont. I've seen lots of agents and I think there is one I like. Here at the Chateau Marmont, Foxy and I have met Beatrice Lillie and her spaniel Lord Buttons. Foxy likes Lord Buttons and has had the odd pee with him at night in their walks, and everything is fine here."

By return mail I got a letter from Brother Frank, who said, "I'm so glad to hear that things seem to be going well for you there. Be very careful in picking your agent. I'm glad that you are comfortable at the Chateau Marmont. I am more than pleased to know that Foxy has made such a celebrated friend as Lord Buttons, but it would seem to me that in the pressing of this career that you so seek it might have been better for you if you had a pee with Bea Lillie."

I was completely charmed by the weather and by just being in Hollywood. I remember one day doing a scene in the Selznick Studio and waiting for my part to begin. The fifty-nine-year old coffee boy pointed out to me that I was standing on the very spot where they'd built the staircase on which Clark Gable had carried Vivien Leigh in *Gone with the Wind*. I probably just stood there with my mouth open! It was extremely entertaining for someone like me, who loves the history of the movies.

A Horse and a Hero

I no sooner got to Hollywood than I found myself transported to a place called Torreón in the middle of Mexico, making a western called *The Hour of the Gun*. This meant riding lots of horses, and I was reminded yet again that I hate horses. Of course, I did a ton of riding in this "duster." I fell off every horse I rode—or the horse turned around and went back to the barn with me on it. It was so embarrassing. ▭

One morning I grudgingly went to get the horse I was assigned for the day. A voice said, "Mr. Willis, I think that you will find this horse nicer. He's gentle and I think you and he will get along."

The man who was speaking was just out of my line of vision. He was very short. I looked down at this little man and said, "I know you. You're Roy Rogers."

He said, "That's right, Mr. Willis. I am."

I said, "What are you doing here at this hour of the morning, giving me a horse?"

He said, "This is what I do. One of my jobs is providing horses for the all the Westerns being shot down here, as I own all these horses."

Austin Willis in an undated photo. Willis had famously bad luck with horses.

So my screen idol gave me a new horse—and it worked out just fine. I never spoke ill of a horse again.

The Real Bad Guys

Mexico was not my favourite place to be working. They had built our Tombstone set forty miles from where we were staying, which meant a hideous taxi ride. Our Mexican drivers prided themselves on going across fields and through farmyards, avoiding roads as much as possible. There were fellows walking around town with bandoliers filled with ammunition—and they weren't actors. We were all pretty terrified. Indeed, we had a gun collector on the film, one of the assistant directors, and he went off to do a gun deal with somebody.

John Wayne, who made a lot of Westerns in Mexico, sent us his personal police force, in the form of a single guy called Raoul. When Raoul hit Torreón the police evaporated—and so did the guys with the bandoliers. We never had another problem. One night the filmmakers took us to a bar full of locals with lots of guns. Raoul would check out the bathroom before we used it to make sure it was safe for us.

On a Lighter Note

In the 1967 film Eight on the Lam, *Bob Hope plays a bank teller; his fiancée is played by Shirley Eaton, and his housekeeper is played by Phyllis Diller.*

Bob Hope was the glib and gleeful iconic American comedian who conquered the realm of radio before moving on to television and film. He was also renowned for his USO shows entertaining troops in battle zones during the Second World War, in Korea, and in Vietnam.

It was then a great relief to be asked to do a comedic (and safe) film with Bob Hope, *Eight on the Lam.* ▢ I played a bank manager with a very sexy girlfriend played by Jill St. John. The teller was found embezzling funds from the bank by the bank's detective, played by Jonathan Winters. I had done a lot of work with Bob overseas during the war, but I hated this script and the part that I played. Still, I couldn't offend Bob Hope—and you didn't say no to any part you were offered in Hollywood. I hope no one ever recognized me in this film. ▢

Waiting and Waiting and Waiting

Waiting in Hollywood to get into your next movie is hideous because you can do nothing to help yourself. You just have to stay home and sit beside your swimming pool (I know—true hardship!). In my case, I made flowerpots out of old barrels, put wheels on them, and planted flowers. In Canada, throughout my entire career, whenever I didn't have something lined up, I would be pounding on somebody's desk, saying, "Don't you know you are looking at the greatest star in the country? I should be working."

At home, at least I could say something to somebody. But in Hollywood if you bothered your agent too much he got angry with you.

I wasn't the only one waiting around. We unemployed Canadians would get together to dream up schemes to occupy our time. One of our "projects" actually came to fruition in *The Joseph File*—a detective story we wrote together, and which was actually published as a book. Alf Harris, our writer from our *Space Command* days, was listed as author because he was the only one who was actually a writer in our group. (I do not expect that anyone will find this in any library any-

Set in Los Angeles, The Joseph File *is a novel that follows Dave Campbell from Kansas as he becomes vice-president of prestigious World Ways Airlines.*

where—though you can check out my copy in the Austin Willis collection at Saint Mary's University.)

As I've mentioned before, when you are in a film you spend a lot of time waiting. I remember playing a character in C.H.O.M.P.S., a Hanna-Barbera film about a robotic dog, directed by Don Chaffey. We sat at a reservoir for two days waiting for this fantastically trained dog to come to his master, but he wouldn't do it. It was costing the company a fortune, as two days is a long time for a production to be idle in Hollywood. Finally, one of the extras made boots for the dog's feet and the dog immediately played his part. Apparently the cement of the reservoir had been too hot for the dog's paws.

Thanks to my friend Rod Taylor, in 1970 I played a businessman whose daughter runs off with a hippie in *Zabriskie Point*. 🎞 We waited impatiently for a full two weeks to get a shot that our director, Michelangelo Antonioni, wanted but never did get of Santa Catalina Island. 🎞

The economics of Hollywood are strange. There can be tremendous waste on some sets, but on others, filmmakers would save money by staging two fights with the same actor playing two different characters—and just change that actor's hat or costume.

Rod Taylor was an Australian actor in stage and radio before coming to Hollywood in the 1950s, where he starred in more than fifty feature films, including The Time Machine *and* The Birds.

Zabriskie Point *was an examination of youth counterculture and Antonioni's first American-shot film— but it proved to be the rare flop of Antonioni's stellar career.*

I certainly made great friends in Hollywood, and I struck up a great relationship with Eddie Foy Jr. and his family when we worked together on *Ten Girls Ago*. When I arrived in Hollywood he took me sightseeing in his convertible, which he loved to drive around wearing a silly hat.

The musician Glen Campbell was another friend. We were together in San Diego on the *Queen Mary*, shooting the pilot of *Casino*, a project that never went anywhere. Glen had a friend who was going to drive him back to Hollywood one night. He asked me if I would drive *his* car back, and I said sure. It was a Jaguar XK-E—one of the ones you practically have to lie down in while driving. I wasn't used to this, as I had never driven one before. I drove down the San Diego freeway reclining so far back in this car, I was a basket case when I got home. 🎞

Glen Campbell was an American musician and actor who rose through the ranks of studio players and eventually had a long career as successful pop vocalist. He hosted a highly rated television variety series—The Glen Campbell Goodtime Hour. He played guitar on hundreds of hit songs with the Wrecking Crew, a loose group of session musicians who worked on thousands of recordings in Los Angeles in the 1960s and '70s. He briefly replaced Brian Wilson in the Beach Boys, and he made "Wichita Lineman" his signature hit.

I have sometimes thought that I may hold the record for being in the most productions that the world has never seen—from the Canadian films that were barely seen in Canada, let alone the rest of the world, to the pilots for television series' that never went anywhere, to my venture into vaudeville at Kleinburg in the early 1960s.

Around Town

Then, while I was living in Hollywood, my agent—bless him—found me a gig introducing people to whatever cities they were visiting. *Around Town with Austin Willis* was a monthly video production seen only in hotel rooms. In Toronto, for example, the bellhop carrying your luggage would turn on the television in your room and I would appear, suggesting what you should do and see in Toronto—over and over again.

It took us some time to shoot our footage in Toronto, and we would add to it every month. Initially I was being paid a penny per day per hotel room where this was available—which actually added up to a handsome income—until the venture was sold to Columbia Pictures, which unilaterally changed the contract. The films were edited in Las Vegas, and I would have to travel there every month. Through this whole project, I grew to absolutely loathe Las Vegas, and I still hate it to this day.

Mind you, Vegas always brought interesting people together; I have one memorable story to share. My great friend Sammy Davis Jr. often appeared in Vegas in those days, and I would always go around and see him when I was in town. One night he offered to take me around to introduce me to Elvis Presley. We watched his performance and I was as giddy as a little girl seeing Elvis Presley perform. But meeting him was very different. Presley was not in a good state then, and my awe of him as performer evaporated when we shook hands. ⌑

The Elvis Presley who performed on stage in Las Vegas in the 1970s was a sad relic of his former self. His health was in decline, he had gained an excessive amount of weight, and he was addicted to pharmaceutical drugs.

Clint's Turtle—Fred

Eventually I bought a house in California's San Fernando Valley, and my next-door neighbour for fourteen years was Clint Eastwood. ⌑ Clint was a wonderful guy. Much like the guy you see on screen, he grunted a lot. He was very sweet to me. He would make little visits to my house. One day he came over and said, "What size are your feet?"

This startled me. I said, "Eleven and a half." He went away, no explanation, no anything. The next day, when I went to leave the house, a shoebox was sitting outside my front door, and in it was a pair of red running shoes, which I still have to this day. They were my size. I never needed another pair of running shoes as long as I lived.

Clint Eastwood was a regular in the TV Westerns of the 1950s before he rose to fame as the star of Sergio Leone's "spaghetti Western" films in the mid-1960s. Famous for his taciturn personal and stage presence, he became a director in the 1970s while Austin was living next door.

Another time Clint knocked on my door and said, "What are you doing? Are you working?"

I said, "I'm not."

He said: "You might as well work for me. I am doing a picture. It will only be a couple of days."

That's how I got into *Firefox*. I am in a fairly long scene with Clint, but it doesn't seem to appear in every edition of the film; I never know whether it will be included in the version that people are seeing. Otherwise, I am

Firefox was a 1982 thriller shot in Austria; it reportedly had a budget of $21 million, of which $20 million was spent on special effects.

just a background extra, but I still get residuals from that one today.

I have worked on a lot of pictures in Hollywood, but Clint Eastwood pictures are very different. When he is directing there is more fun, more laughter. Everything is light and bubbly. Also, the food is marvellous. On other pictures, the caterer comes at breakfast, lunch, and supper—and they go away in between. On his films, the caterer was with us all day long. We had lobster, shrimp, anything. People got fat on Clint's pictures.

Clint loved animals of all sorts. He had a turtle at home named Fred, who would sometimes get away from him. He would call me and say, "Fred's run away."

So I would have to go look for Fred, because if Clint went looking, people would want to talk to him. He didn't like that, so I would go find Fred and bring him back home. Sometimes Fred would wind up in my pool and I would have to dive in and get him. Fred became quite a nuisance.

My final Clint Eastwood story involves a tiny bottle of brandy that I had brought from my days in Europe. I would hardly drink it myself, or offer it to anyone, because it was so wonderful—and so expensive. One night there was a knock on the door (when Clint came to the door, all I ever saw was his belt buckle, because he is so tall). I opened the door and he had this great big measuring cup in his hand and he said, "Austin, Sarah's cooking. She needs some brandy."

The only brandy I had was this marvellous bottle. Into his enormous measuring cup I poured maybe half an inch. He never moved the cup. He just kept it right there.

"More?" I asked.

He said, "She needs a cup."

I gave him a cup of this glorious brandy and off he went. Eventually I figured that, between finding Fred and donating the cup of brandy, I had paid for the fancy running shoes.

ELEVEN

Hollywood Was a Mistake

"If you don't like the heat, get out of the kitchen," goes the old saying.

By 1970, I realized I had to get out of the Hollywood kitchen. The long waits between parts really got to me, as well as taking those parts I didn't like because I had to work—but I had to eat.

I called my agent one day and said, "Walt, I can't stand this. I've made two thousand birdhouses and I've painted twenty-seven barrels. Put me in television."

"Austin," he said, "you know if you go into television you are not going to be in movies again."

I said, "Never mind; I'll go into television."

So I did. I made four zillion television shows.▣ My onscreen

Austin Willis played in two episodes of the NBC television series I Spy; he had guest roles in the television series' The FBI, Run for Your Life, Cannon, and The Rat Patrol; in the courtroom drama Judd for the Defense; as a doctor in two episodes of Mannix; back in space with The Invaders; and in the made-for-television films The Sheriff and Death Takes a Holiday.

credit was often above the titles—a sign that I was doing well. In fact, I was doing better than I had done in movies.

When the opportunity arose, I couldn't refuse the chance to go fishing with Blake Emmons on his CFTO television show *Fish 'N Stars* back in Toronto. I was living in California at the time, so I flew to Toronto, got on another plane, and flew to Thunder Bay. I got off that plane and boarded another one and flew somewhere else—then I got on a fourth plane with pontoons on it. We flew over landscapes where there was nothing below but forest fires that had been caused by lightning. We finally landed, and when I arrived at the lodge the sign on my door said, "Keep Closed—Be Aware of Bears." The bathroom facility was one two-holer for twelve people. This was the luxurious accommodation Emmons had promised me.

Blake Emmons was a Canadian country music singer, actor, and host whose roles include hosting the Playboy Shopping Show, a live daily show on the Playboy Network.

I had two huge suitcases with me. In one was a white dinner jacket that would clearly never be worn here. I never stopped abusing Emmons and received a lot of good-natured abuse in return.

We would go out in two boats. The cameraman was in a little boat with an outboard engine, and Blake, with whichever "star" had joined him, was in the other. We would fish for three days wearing microphones—no prepared dialogue, no anything. They recorded all of it, then edited the footage and audio together to make a show. They got some very good shows out of this scenario, but, as you can imagine, it was kind of hit-and-miss.

But I hadn't gone to Hollywood to work in television. Working in Hollywood was very different from what I had done at home in Canada, where I was used to doing radio, doing theatre, doing television, doing it all. When I grumble about Hollywood, that's what I mean.

Austin Willis (left) fishing with Blake Emmons in Fish 'N Stars, *1977.*

Back to Canada

I was always running back and forth to Toronto during my period in Hollywood, which made things difficult for my film career. I was keeping my hand in back home and never said no to any opportunity. I was in a couple of episodes of *Adventures in Rainbow Country*, once as a visiting tourist and another time a famous journalist.[□] Indeed, *Rainbow Country* brings to mind the most bizarre reaction I ever had to one of my guest roles. I was playing a millionaire tourist catching a fish—which went smoothly, I thought. Then I got a phone call after the pilot telling me that I was the worst damn actor on the face of the earth. I was stunned and asked what was wrong—they said it was obvious that the bloody fish was dead!

> *Adventures in Rainbow Country was a* CBC-TV *drama series set in Northern Ontario and broadcast in 1970 and 1971.*

I did lots of telethons in my day, and I remember working with everybody from author and journalist Pierre Berton to jazz musician Guido Basso to singer Tommy Ambrose to famed wrestler Whipper Billy Watson—and I could tell you stories about all of them, but in the interest of discretion I won't. At the beginning of Canada's centennial year I also hosted a CBC variety special called *100 Years Young.* ▣

> *100 Years Young was a ninety-minute television extravaganza headlined by comedy duo Wayne and Shuster; it included performances by everyone from singer Juliette to impressionist Rich Little and featured Gordon Lightfoot singing "Canadian Railroad Trilogy," a song that had been commissioned by the CBC to mark the Centennial.*

Being a Target—Again

In 1977 got myself involved with initiating, researching, and hosting a syndicated television series called *So the Story Goes.* Each episode dramatized a historical story and was shot at the location where the story originated. I've always been a storyteller, and I completely enjoyed telling the stories behind everything from "four and twenty blackbirds" to Scotland's Melville Castle to the tale of Robin Hood. We made some twenty-six episodes that made their way to limited American markets. ▣

We shot the story of Robin Hood—where else?—in the Sherwood Forest in Nottinghamshire, England, beside "The Major Oak," which was said to be the shelter for Robin Hood and his Merry Men. Of course, we had to have an arrow go zinging past my head into the tree. For this, we hired the champion archer of England, a strapping

> *So the Story Goes was produced by Panda-Tillicum Productions in 1977 and broadcast by CHCH–Toronto, CKPR–Thunder Bay, CHEX–Peterborough, CKND–Winnipeg, CFAC–Calgary, CITV–Edmonton, in eight American markets, and by US Armed Forces at their overseas bases.*

eighteen-year-old fellow. He had a longbow that was twice as big as he was.

I asked, "May I see you fire a few arrows?"

It was remarkable how accurate he was. He could shoot cans out of trees. But we still had to get him to shoot an arrow close to my head. He was pretty close to me when he fired—the angle of the camera helped with the illusion, and I was never in real danger—but he had to do it twice because I shut my eyes tight the first time and blinked the second time. In the end, we had to use the take where I blinked.

Maintaining the Law

I had had a great relationship with *Front Page Challenge* over the years, and I was rumored to be in the running to host the show after its first season, but I was too busy to commit to that in those days. I did become a perennial guest panellist whenever a scheduled panellist couldn't make it—when I was available.

In 1971 the CBC developed a game show spinoff from *Front Page Challenge* called *This Is The Law,* and I became the host for the length of its run. Paul Soles had just had a great success at Stratford playing Shylock in *The Merchant of Venice.*

This Is The Law was great fun, and anyone who remembers me likely does so because of this

Front Page Challenge *was a very successful* CBC *Television game show that ran from 1957 to 1995 and was hosted by Fred Davis. Pierre Berton, Betty Kennedy, and Gordon Sinclair were the regular panellists and, together with a guest panellist, they had to figure out the identity of the hidden guest associated with a news story.*

Each episode of This Is The Law *began with a short dramatic vignette in which Paul Soles played a character who broke an obscure law and Robert Warner played the policeman who would arrest him. Panellists had to figure out which law had been broken in the scene.* This Is The Law *aired from 1971 to 1976 on the* CBC.

show. It was a great show to be remembered for—though I always believed that making movies was more important.

Being host means you are always acting, always gracious, and always encouraging everyone around you—and I would like to think that I was good at this. This is why I am perfectly delighted when the ladies at the shopping centre remember me from *This Is The Law*. It was great fun to do and afforded our guest panellists an opportunity to show off their wit and charm—and we had a good long run with it.

MONDAYS, 8:30 PM

CBC TELEVISION

Austin Willis (centre) with his celebrated panel and his celebrated lawbreaker (right) in This Is The Law, *1971–1979.*

Austin Willis as the gracious host of This Is The Law, *1971–1979.*

TWELVE

Who's Austin Willis?

My final appearance in Canadian film was in *The Boy in Blue*, which we shot around Smiths Falls, Ontario, in the mid-1980s. I played a mean and nasty character in a stovepipe hat—a character I didn't enjoy playing very much. Indeed, we got a withering review in the *New York Times*. [𝄢]

But that's where I met Gwen, who came on the picture as an extra. She looked really tremendous in the costumes of the day—and still looks tremendous today. I am very blessed to have

The Boy in Blue *told the story of Ned Hanlan, the nineteenth-century sculler, and starred Nicolas Cage, Christopher Plummer, Cynthia Dale, and Melody Anderson. It was directed by Charles Jarrott and released in 1986. Nina Darnton, in the* New York Times, *described* The Boy in Blue *as a "witless, tedious contrivance" full of "stereotypes" and "unimaginative and corny dialogue." Fortunately, she made no mention of Austin Willis whatsoever.*

been able to return to my home in Nova Scotia; thanks to my marvellous wife, Gwen, for bringing me home. ⊡ She looks after all my needs, especially my need for laughter, with such loving care.

Austin Willis married Gwen Laforty in 1995 and they lived in Wetaskiwin, Alberta, before moving to Halifax in 1998 and renting a home in Dartmouth. They also purchased a summer home in Margaretsville, Nova Scotia, on the Bay of Fundy.

When I first moved to Dartmouth, I was walking down the hallway at a shopping mall when a woman appeared in front of me and said, "Didn't you used to be Austin Willis?"

I said, "Yes, madam, but a very long time ago."

Then Costas found me—and he and Ern convinced me to talk about who this Austin Willis was. I agreed to come to King's Theatre in Annapolis Royal to do a one-man show because it was a very small theatre, out of the way. If I fell flat on my face, no one was going to hear me—it was a tryout. They ran out of tape, recording my presentation. At least, that's what Ern told me— maybe to justify him asking his questions over and over again.

I do wonder what Brother Frank would think.

Brother Frank never got such an opportunity as this—he died at the age of sixty. He would have had so much to say about broadcasting and everything else but was too involved in the day-to-day opportunities to reflect on our evolving media. He was always so careful and so articulate that I can't imagine what he would make of digital—and instantaneous— everything these days. Many books and documentaries have memorialized his role reporting for radio from the Moose River mine disaster, but he would have had more to say if he had lived to my ripe old age. And I do miss his asides—always keeping me humble. ⊡

A small J. Frank Willis collection was assembled from Austin Willis's holdings and has been deposited at the Saint Mary's University Archives. A fellow Nova Scotian, Bill MacNeil, did a eulogy for Willis on CBC Radio that can be heard at cbc.ca/archives/ entry/a-eulogy-for-j-frank-willis.

Brother Frank—J. Frank Willis—during his groundbreaking live broadcast of the Moose River mine disaster, 1936.

Final Confessions

I have some final confessions that I had best get off my chest.

This head of hair of mine has been both a curse and a blessing. I went white when I was twenty-two as a reaction to some sort of dye they were using on my head for a particular stage production. First my own hair turned green, and when I shaved it off that left me with a green halo. But my hair grew back snow white, though as wavy as ever—and my hair led me to lots of roles that required this look.

Another: after my harrowing experience playing a Roman centurion in *The Barbarians*, I had come back to Toronto, and Brother Frank called me one night after seeing me on television. He told me the bags under my eyes were right down to my knees.

"You are going to have to do something. The makeup does not do a thing."

So I went to see a fellow who was the doctor for the Toronto Maple Leafs. He worked for an hour and a half on each eye, without putting me under. He froze the area and I never felt a thing, but I could see the knife coming at me. After the surgery I looked like a raccoon from the bruising—so I had to wear dark glasses everywhere for a couple of weeks.

Right at this time I got a wonderful surprise as I was called to go to New York to do a reading for the play *Man and Boy* with Charles Boyer, which was opening in London and then playing in New York. There must have been a hundred or more people at this reading with Charles and me. I was asked to take my glasses off and I resisted, explaining that I had had an operation to have the bags taken off underneath my eyes. This only prompted great curiosity, and everyone gathered around me. We never did do the reading but went straight to lunch to discuss the surgery further. Thus began a string of people travelling to Toronto to have their bags removed, as the doctor there apparently was using a new procedure that left no traces.

To this day, my face hasn't aged. That should show Brother Frank—who is surely looking down on me now, as he always did.

Goodbye

I should let you get on with your life and rest from this long look at my life. It was certainly a busy go—sixty years since I left Nova Scotia. I had a good kick at the can, really. There were sad patches, but also great fun times—and I certainly remember both.

I will leave you with this picture in your mind's eye: I've just arrived in Dartmouth and am moving into my house. As the golf clubs come in from the truck, a twelve-year-old comes up onto the stoop and says that he has seen me on TV. I doubt that but expect that his parents have explained who is moving into their neighbourhood. He says he will be glad to play golf with me anytime. He then retires to his bike on the sidewalk and settles down to watch the movers.

A second twelve-year-old rides up on his bike and joins him. My new friend very smartly says, "Would you like to meet Austin Willis?"

The new arrival looks all around and says, "Who's Austin Willis?" Now you know! ▢

The audiences attending An Evening with Austin Willis *at King's Theatre in Annapolis Royal and at Convocation Hall at Saint Mary's University stood and cheered and cried and clapped for Austin Willis at the end of his performance.*

Austin Willis—Pioneer, Journeyman, and Friend

by RON FOLEY MACDONALD

For me, the stories and work of Austin Willis provide a road map—a constellation, perhaps, is the better word—to the twentieth century's long and twisting course through an evolving mass media in three of the countries that practiced mass media par excellence. Not only did Austin Willis literally grow up with radio; he was part of the birth of television in Canada, and he managed to preside over one of the world's first coast-to-coast broadcasts (like his beloved brother, J. Frank Willis, who executed the first live disaster broadcast at the Moose River mine disaster in 1936). This avuncular ocean of charm and character was also, in fact, something of a broadcasting pioneer.

Austin Willis was not simply following in the footsteps of two earlier Halifax-born big screen stars: David Manners and Ruby Keeler. He was exploring a much wider universe where electronic media expanded from the audio-only margins of radio to the full-on invasion of domestic North American living rooms by television. By the time of the early 1970s and the CBC program *This Is The Law*, Austin Willis was ubiquitous, with his widely recognizable visage making him something of a Canadian icon.

Austin Willis had a more important career in film than I'd imagined. Despite a short burst in the mid-1980s of the so-called "Toronto New Wave" (Atom Egoyan, Patricia Rozema, John Greyson, Ron Mann, Bruce McDonald), English Canada's cinema culture has never truly taken off. This, however, never stopped Austin Willis, who went on acting in film, radio, and television—Canadian, British, and American. He had a peculiar knack for appearing in supporting roles in films by some of the world's most famous directors—Antonioni, John Sturges, Clint Eastwood, Richard Fleischer. Strangely, though, Austin Willis always ended up in the less famous films—*Zabriski Point* rather than *Blow Up* by Michelangelo Antonioni, *Hour of the Gun* by John Sturges rather than *The Magnificent Seven*, and *Crack in the Mirror* instead of 20,000 *Leagues Under the Sea* by Richard Fleischer.

Austin Willis was a journeyman actor. And what a journey! Theatre in London, England; television in Toronto and Los Angeles; a string of film appearances in internationally successful landmark feature films such as Jack Arnold's 1960 comedy masterpiece *The Mouse That Roared* and Richard Fleischer's multiscreen, true-crime, 1968 epic *The Boston Strangler*.

Austin Willis did inventive things in a conservative, self-deprecating way. It's a typical East Coast way of doing things, like his fellow artists: the director Daniel Petrie (who chose unconventional subject matter for his films—race relations in *A Raisin in the Sun*, contemporary morality in *Eleanor and Franklin*, for example) or Alex Colville, an even better example, whose work of almost clinical realism explored lyricism and violence often side by side.

Willis not only pursued a career in acting, he attempted to jump-start the nascent Canadian film industry in 1946 and 1948 when there simply was no Canadian film industry. Failing that, the shock-haired thespian continued to show up in other Canadians' work when they tried to do the same things he had. In the newspaper reports of then-emerging director Sidney J. Furie as he somehow made the late-1950s Toronto-shot feature film *The Dangerous Age*—starring Austin Willis in a crucial role of the police authority figure—you can see the age-old struggle of English Canada's futile strivings to carve out its own cinema culture. That moving picture image of ourselves is still so elusive.

As Austin relates earlier in this book, some Nova Scotian wag remarked, upon seeing him at a grocery store: "Didn't you used to be Austin Willis?" Fame, in the latter day mass media world, has both drawbacks and advantages. For Austin Willis, it was all part of simply making a living.

But in that constellation—the stars in the pantheon or the sky—once you start to connect those dots you can draw a unique and startling picture of a life and a career that touched the skies of a mass media universe that was, for the most part, shockingly new and still not widely understood. And Austin Willis saw it all, taking it all in and never losing his charm or self-depreciating humour.

From the bridge of the *Bluenose* at its last race for the International Fisherman's Cup in 1938, to the soundstages of Hollywood and Pinewood Studios outside of London, to King's Theatre in Annapolis Royal and Saint Mary's University in Nova Scotia, Austin Willis has always projected his smooth-as-silk baritone and old-world sophistication.

The world is a better place for Austin Willis—and I am better person for having been his friend.

Austin Willis Timeline

1917

- Born September 20 in Halifax. The Willis family sold and distributed pianos made by Willis & Co. in Montreal.

1933

- Attended King's College School, Windsor, Nova Scotia.

1936

- Older brother, J. Frank Willis, pioneered live radio news reporting when he covered the story of three men trapped underground at Moose River, Nova Scotia, for the Canadian Radio Broadcasting Commission, forerunner of the CBC.
- Contributed to CHNS.

1937

- Joined CBC in Halifax.

1939

- Moved to Toronto to work for CBC Radio.

1940

- Joined the John Holden Players, Bala, Ontario, for the summer season.
- Hosted *Carry On Canada!*, a weekly CBC Radio program that encouraged Canadians to support the war effort.
- Hosted the CBC Radio weekly series *They Shall Not Pass*, reporting Second World War battles in Britain.
- Hosted *The Life Line Holds*, a CBC Radio series produced by J. Frank Willis about the Royal Canadian Navy.

1940, 1942, 1945

- Commentator on CBC Radio's *Children's Scrapbook*, written by Mary Grannan.

1941

- Joined the Royal Canadian Navy.
- Announcer and host on CBC Radio's *War Savings Broadcast*.
- Announcer for weekly live CBC Radio drama series *John and Judy*.

1941, 1945

* Hosted the weekly CBC Radio series *Voice of Victor*, written by Arch Oboler and sponsored by RCA Victor.

1941, 1942, 1943

* Announcer and host on CBC Radio's *Victory Loan Hour*, which raised money for Canada's war effort.

1942

* Announcer for CBC Radio documentary *British Commonwealth: Newfoundland*.
* Announcer for *Canada Marches*, a CBC Radio series dramatizing the history of the Canadian army, written by Alan King.
* Commentator for the CBC Radio special *Christmas is a Promise*, written by Fletcher Markle.
* Host of the CBC Radio program *All Star Variety Show*, on behalf of the second Victory Loan campaign.

1942, 1944

* Hosted *Fighting Navy*, a CBC Radio weekly series written and produced by William Strange.
* Performed in *Comrades in Arms*, a CBC Radio weekly series produced by J. Frank Willis.

1942, 1943

* Narrated *The People*, a radio drama written by Len Peterson.

1943, 1944

- Host and announcer for *Victory Star Show*, a live CBC Radio broadcast from Massey Hall in Toronto promoting Canada's war effort.

1944

- Reported from Britain on the progress of the Second World War for CBC Radio.
- Hosted *Hot Stove League* for Imperial Oil; the radio show ran between periods of National Hockey League broadcasts from Toronto.

1945

- Played an aspiring pianist on the CBC Radio drama *Hometown*, directed by Bernard Braden.
- Acted in *Soldier's Wife*, a soap opera on CBC Radio.
- Acted in the CBC Radio dramatic series *Curtain Time*.
- Performed in *Purity Flour Show*, a CBC Radio program.
- Acted in the CBC Radio drama *Mulrooney's New Year's Party*.
- Performed in *Evening Scrapbook* on CBC Radio.

1946

- Invested in, organized, and played the lead in *Bush Pilot*, a Canadian feature film also starring Jack La Rue and Rochelle Hudson.
- Performed in *Johnny Home Show*, a weekly radio series on CBC produced by J. Frank Willis.

1947

- Narrated a dramatization of the legend of the Dutch ship *Flying Dutchman* for the CBC Radio series *It's a Legend*.

1948

- Played the role of a public health officer in the Canadian feature film *Sins of the Fathers*.
- Acted in the radio drama "The Book of Job" for the series CBC *Wednesday Night*.

1949

- Narrated the radio drama "The Rich Man" on CBC *Wednesday Night*.
- Narrated the "Everyman" episode of the radio drama series CBC *Wednesday Night*.
- Acted in "Peter Grimes," a radio opera written by Benjamin Britten for the series CBC *Wednesday Night*.
- Acted in the radio drama "The Seven Who Were Hanged" on CBC *Wednesday Night*.

1950

- Played a lawyer in the stage production of *Detective Story* at The Princes Theatre in London.
- Narrated *Glimpses of Britain* for CBC Radio.

1950, 1951

- Narrated the CBC Radio play "The Plouffe Family," broadcast as part of the *Stage 51* series.

1951

- Acted in the radio drama "The Flower in the Rock," directed by Andrew Allan for the CBC series *Stage 51*.

1951, 1953–1957, 1961

- Host and producer of the CBC Radio program *Of All Things*, which featured light recorded music and chit-chat.

1953, 1954

- Played the commander in the CBC Television series *Space Command*.
- Acted in the "Hometown Laughter" episode of *Jake and the Kid* for CBC Radio.

1954

- Married Kate Reid; son, Reid, born.
- Acted in the CBC Television dramatic comedy "The Big Leap," broadcast as part of the series *General Motors Theatre*.
- Narrated the radio drama "The Great Eastern," produced by J. Frank Willis, on CBC *Wednesday Night*.
- Alternated with Fred Davis as host of an NFB documentary series for CBC Television called *On the Spot*.

1955–1957

- Hosted the weekly half-hour musical variety CBC Television program *Cross-Canada Hit Parade*.
- Acted in "The Sand Castle," an original comedy for the CBC Television series *General Motors Theatre*.

- Acted in the stage production of *The Moon is Blue* at the Garden Centre Theatre in Toronto.
- Acted in the stage production of *Laura* at the Garden Centre Theatre in Toronto.

1956

- Acted in the radio drama "Groundswell" in the CBC *Stage* series.

1957

- Moved to London, England, with Kate Reid and son.
- Played an aging hockey player in "Ice on Fire," an episode of the CBC Television dramatic series *First Performance*.
- Acted in the CBC *Television Theatre* drama "The Birthday Party," written by Arthur Kavanagh.
- Played a police official in the Canadian feature film *A Dangerous Age*, directed by Sidney Furie and featuring Kate Reid.
- Acted in the CBC Television drama *Friend of the People*, written by Mordecai Richler.
- Played the villain in the Canadian feature film *Wolf Dog*, also known as *A Boy and His Dog*, shot in and around Markdale, Ontario.
- Played the estranged husband (whose wife was played by Kate Reid) in "Reunion" for the CBC Television dramatic series *On Camera*.

1957, 1958

- Played Mr. Chadwick in the long-running stage comedy *Roar Like a Dove* at the Phoenix Theatre in London, England.

1957, 1960

- Guest panellist on the CBC Television series *Front Page Challenge,* hosted by Fred Davis, with Pierre Berton, Betty Kennedy, and Gordon Sinclair.

1958

- Daughter, Robin, born.
- Acted in the "Hudson's Bay" episode of *Voice in the Wilderness,* a dramatic thirty-nine-part television series filmed at Kleinburg, Ontario.
- Played a doctor in the comedy "A Cure for the Doctor" for the CBC Television series *On Camera.*
- Interviewed Christopher Plummer on the CBC Radio program *Canadian Scene.*

1959

- Played the US Secretary of Defense in the British feature film *The Mouse That Roared,* a satirical comedy with Peter Sellers, Jean Seberg, and William Hartnell.
- Hosted an episode of the CBC Television public affairs series *Close-Up.*
- Played a Royal Canadian Navy Commander in the CBC Television drama "A Leap in the Dark" on the series *General Motors Presents.*
- Acted in the stage play *Tunnel of Love* at Lansdowne Theatre in Toronto.

1959–1963

- Hosted the daily radio series *Matinée with Willis*, sponsored by Matinée cigarettes and heard on private radio stations across Canada.

1960

- Played a supporting role in the American feature film *Crack in the Mirror*.
- Acted in the television drama "You Win, You Lose" on *General Motors Theatre*.
- Acted in the CBC Television drama "Madge is for Maybe" on *General Motors Theatre*.
- Guest on CBLT *Birthday Party*, a celebration of eight years of television.
- Acted in the CBC Television drama "The Night They Killed Joe Howe" for *General Motors Theatre*.
- Acted in the CBC Television drama "Hide Me In the Mountains" for *General Motors Theatre*.
- Acted in "The Hero At Home," an episode of the CBC Television series *Explorations*.
- Acted in "Collision" for the CBC series *General Motors Theatre*.
- Played a supporting role in the black and white dramatic feature film *I Aim at the Stars*, about Nazi missile scientist Wernher von Braun.
- Played the father of a delinquent girl in *Too Young to Love*, a British black and white feature film.
- Played a Roman centurion in the pilot for the dramatic series *Rivak the Barbarian*, also known as *The Barbarians*.
- Played the lead male role in the stage play *The Marriage-Go-Round* for Crest Theatre in Toronto.

1961

- Played a charming seducer in the feature film *Exploring the Kinsey Reports*, also known as 1 + 1, directed and produced by Arch Oboler and featuring Kate Reid.
- Acted in the British comedy film *Upstairs and Downstairs*, directed by Ralph Thomas.
- Played a jail governor in the television adaptation of the Brendan Behan play "The Quare Fellow" in the CBC series *Festival*.
- Led the cast of the television drama "Counsel for the Defense" for the CBC series *General Motors Presents*.
- Played the lead male role in the matrimonial farce *The Marriage-Go-Round* for the Straw Hat Players in theatres across Ontario during the summer of 1961.
- Acted in the television drama "Company Party" for the CBC series *General Motors Theatre*.
- Voiced the documentary "Enchanted Village" with other actors for the CBC Television series *Camera Canada*.
- Acted in the radio drama "Alexandra's Island" for the series *CBC Stage*.
- Performed in the stage play *Simon Says Get Married*, written by Bernard Slade and performed at Crest Theatre in Toronto.

1962

- Played a hapless TV news director in *Ten Girls Ago*, an incomplete Canadian film that satirized television.
- Performed in the television drama "The Origin of the Species" on the CBC series *Playdate*.
- Acted in "The Looking Glass World" on the CBC series *Playdate*.

- Hosted the CBC Television program *From Here to '63*.
- Played a symphony conductor in the stage play *Once More With Feeling*, directed by John Holden and performed at the Manitoba Theatre Centre in Winnipeg.
- Lead actor in the stage play *Jason* at the Crest Theatre in Toronto.

1963

- Performed in "The Last Illusion," an episode of the CBS dramatic television series *The Defenders*.
- Played an American tycoon in the stage play *Man and Boy* in Brighton, England, and later on Broadway.
- Led the cast in "The Man Who Cheered the Leafs" for the CBC Television series *Playdate*.

1964

- Played Simmons, a character who played cards against Auric Goldfinger at Miami Beach's Hotel Fontainebleau, in the feature film *Goldfinger*.
- Acted in a six-part dramatization for television of the Morley Callaghan novel *More Joy in Heaven* for CBC Television series *The Serial*.
- Acted in the television drama "Neighbours" for the CBC series *Show of the Week*.
- Played Alexander Galt, with other actors playing the other Fathers of Confederation, retracing a trip from Quebec City to Charlottetown.

1965

- Host and narrator of the CBC Radio series *A Story to Remember*.
- Acted in the two-part television drama "Who Needs an Enemy?" on the CBC series *Show of the Week*.
- Narrated the radio documentary "The Four Jameses" for CBC *Sunday Night*, produced and directed by J. Frank Willis.
- Acted in a five-part espionage melodrama for television, "The Reluctant Agent," for the CBC series *The Serial*.
- Performed in the television drama "Two Terrible Women" for the CBC series *Festival*.
- Acted in the television drama "Whatever Happened to Jeremiah Goodwin?" for the CBC series *Show of the Week*.

1966

- Moved to Hollywood.
- Played General Shaw in "Father Abraham," a two-part episode of the NBC television series *I Spy*.
- Played Warden Mark James in "Anatomy of Prison Break," an episode of the ABC television series *The FBI*, which aired from 1967 to 1974.
- Played a guest role in "The Hour Glass Raid," an episode of the ABC television dramatic Second World War series *The Rat Patrol*.

1966–1967

- Played Admiral Henry Victor Leslie Fox on the CBC Television dramatic series *Seaway*.

1967

- Played a bank manager in the Hollywood comedy film *Eight on the Lam* with Bob Hope, Phyllis Diller, Jonathan Winters, Jill St. John, and Shirley Eaton.
- Played a sheriff in the feature film *Hour of the Gun*, shot in Mexico and directed by John Sturges.
- Hosted the CBC variety special *100 Years Young*, celebrating the beginning of Canada's centennial year.
- Acted in an episode of the ABC television courtroom drama *Judd*, also known as *Judd for the Defense*, broadcast from 1967 to 1969.
- Played the father of a rebellious son in the stage play *A Minor Adjustment*, also known as *Like Father, Like Son*, at the Brooks Atkinson Theatre on Broadway in New York City.
- Hosted a daily five-minute series for CFRB radio, *Stories to Remember*, sponsored by Matinée cigarettes.

1968

- Played a psychiatrist, with a cast that included Tony Curtis, Henry Fonda, and Sally Kellerman, in the feature film *Boston Strangler*, directed by Richard Fleischer.
- Performed in an episode of *Run for Your Life*, an NBC dramatic television series broadcast from 1965 to 1968.
- Played Dr. Mark Gregory in "Who Will Dig the Graves?" and "Deadfall," episodes of the CBS dramatic series *Mannix*, broadcast from 1967 to 1975.
- Played William Gehrig in an episode of the ABC space adventure series *The Invaders*, broadcast in 1967 and 1968.

1969

- Brother J. Frank Willis died in Toronto at the age of sixty.
- Acted in "McQueen The Auctioneer," a television drama in the CBC series *All the World's a Stage*.
- Hosted and invested in *Around Town with Austin Willis*, a series shown in hotel rooms from 1969 to 1972.

1970

- Played Dean Cantwell in *Dr. Frankenstein on Campus*, also known as *Dr. Frankenstein Goes to College*.
- Played a businessman in the feature film *Zabriskie Point*, directed by Michelangelo Antonioni.

1971

- Played the owner of a hockey team in the Canadian feature film *Face-Off*, also known as *Winter Comes Early*, directed by George McCowan.
- Played a judge in the made-for-television movie *The Sheriff*.
- Acted in the made-for-television movie *Death Takes a Holiday*.
- Performed in two episodes of the CBC dramatic television series *Adventures in Rainbow Country*.

1971–1979

- Hosted the CBC Television game show *This Is The Law*.

1975

- Performed in "Coffin Corner," an episode of the CBS dramatic crime series *Cannon*.

1975–1979

* Initiated, researched, and hosted the twenty-six-part syndicated television series *So the Story Goes*.

1977

* Guest celebrity on an episode of *Fish 'N Stars*, a television series developed by Blake Emmons and produced by CFTO from 1976 to 1978.

1978

* Guest host on an episode of the CBC Television psychic game show *Beyond Reason*.

1979

* Acted in the pilot for the television series *Casino*, which was shot on the *Queen Mary*.
* Played an engineer in the feature film C.H.O.M.P.S.

1980

* Played a supporting role in the Hollywood feature film *The Last Flight of Noah's Ark*.

1981

* Played Warren Michaels in "Backlash," an episode of *Vegas*, a television series broadcast from 1978 to 1981.

1982

- Played Walters in the techno-thriller feature film *Firefox*, directed by and starring Clint Eastwood.
- Played a supporting role in the Canadian feature film *The Boy in Blue*, starring Nicolas Cage and Christopher Plummer, released in 1986.

1983

- Acted in the play *The Memory of Murder*, broadcast on the CBC Radio series *Sunday Matinee*.

1985

- Played Senator Willis in *Kane & Abel*, a television miniseries.

1986

- Acted in "The Eyes of Ra," an episode of the CBC Television series *Seeing Things*.

1987

- Moved to Wetaskawin, Alberta.

1992

- Attended a tribute evening held in his honour at the Variety Club, Edmonton; received the Golden Heart Award.

1993

- Kate Reid died in Stratford, Ontario, at the age of sixty-two.

1995

- Married Gwen Laforty.

1996, 1997, 1998

- Interviewed Second World War veterans for the television series *Comrades in Arms*, produced by the video production unit of Veterans Affairs Canada.

1998

- Moved to Dartmouth, Nova Scotia.

1999

- Presented *An Evening with Austin Willis* onstage at King's Theatre, Annapolis Royal, Nova Scotia.

2000

- Presented *An Evening with Austin Willis* at Convocation Hall, Saint Mary's University, Halifax.

2001

- Presented at the closing banquet of "Putting it on Ice," a colloquium on hockey sponsored by the Gorsebrook Research Institute at Saint Mary's University.

2002

- Was awarded an honorary doctorate by Saint Mary's University.
- Received Queen Elizabeth II's Golden Jubilee Medal.
- Received Order of Canada.

2004

- Died April 3 at Dartmouth General Hospital.
- Inducted into the Canadian Broadcast Hall of Fame at the annual meeting of the Canadian Association of Broadcasters in Ottawa.

Acknowledgements

Austin Willis possessed very few copies of his own playbills or publicity shots and had few recordings of the programs and films he had appeared in. But as a film and broadcasting archivist, I knew who to ask to find them, and archivists from Los Angeles to Library and Archives Canada were happy to send us copies of what they had. Librarians everywhere found us references that I did not know of. Particularly, Deborah Lindsay and Doug Kirby at the CBC found us programming that prompted further stories that had been long forgotten.

Resources that I referenced many times include the CBC Radio drama scripts at the Centre for Broadcasting and Journalism Studies at Concordia University, and the listing of CBC network television programming from 1952 to 1982 at Queen's University. Neither have been fully digitized, and no doubt both contain further titles for Austin Willis that I was not able to follow up with. Similarly, the CBC weekly and monthly program schedules from 1948 to 1998 have not been digitized and would definitely yield further references for Austin Willis. Researching digital resources did yield fascinating leads but also conspicuous gaps for his Canadian career.

Margaret Hume interviewed Austin Willis at some length about Austin and his brother, J. Frank Willis, and their complicated relations with Mary Grannan for her book, *Just Mary: The Life of Mary Evelyn Grannan* (Dundurn Press, 2006). She sent us complete transcripts of her interviews, which have been extensively used in constructing this oral memoir of Austin Willis.

Austin Willis had brought with him to Dartmouth a small collection of brother J. Frank Willis's memorabilia that he had carefully tended over the thirty years since the iconic broadcaster had died. Indeed, J. Frank Willis's paintings of maritime scenes adorned Austin's home in Dartmouth—signalling Austin Willis's reverence for his older brother.

Everything is now organized and available for research at the Saint Mary's University Archives—and Austin Willis was so pleased to know that. Indeed, Hansel Cook, University Archivist at Saint Mary's University, has been most helpful in facilitating this book—and in providing the images—and looks forward to further queries about the Austin Wills or J. Frank Willis collections. All royalties from this telling of his story will be donated to the Saint Mary's University Archives to facilitate the ongoing preservation of and access to their collections.

Colin Howell, a pre-eminent historian at Saint Mary's University, also became a great supporter of Austin Willis and found resources to put together the video introduction hosted by Costas Halavrezos (available through the SMU Archives) that serves as a wonderful supplement to this book.[□] I also expect that Colin recommended Austin for the honorary doctorate at Saint Mary's University and the Order of Canada that Austin Willis was awarded in 2002.

Interested readers can download this short documentary by going to tinyurl.com/tmqffpa.

Austin Willis was also inducted in the Canadian Broadcasting Hall of Fame at the annual meeting of the Canadian Association of Broadcasters in 2004, thanks to Kealy Wilkinson of the Canadian Broadcast Museum Foundation.

The most important thank you has to go to Gwen Laforty Willis, Austin's wife, who brought him back to Nova Scotia in 1998. Gwen graciously hosted anyone who wanted to query Austin and then drove him to whatever dinner parties or events we organized for him. Gwen also brought more memorabilia back to their home in Dartmouth than Austin realized and has completed the donation of his collection to Saint Mary's University.

Austin Willis invariably assumed that I knew more than I did, and he prompted me to do much further research following the names and projects he mentioned so casually. Assuming that audiences and readers these days might equally need context, I have assembled my research and Ron Foley Macdonald's formidable understanding into the sidebars that will hopefully help the reader fully appreciate what Austin Willis was trying to tell us.

Thanks to Ron for helping with this context and for helping with dozens of my projects over the years. No one has such wide-ranging experience and understanding of film, television, and performance, and I have relied on him more than anyone knows.

Great thanks go to Angela Mombourquette for her kind and careful editing of this book. I have always appreciated careful editing, and Angela and I share a special bond in documenting the ephemerality of broadcasting and performance. Angela absolutely improved my grammar, spelling, and some of the facts, which I have become confused about over the years, and I look forward to working with her again.

Finally, thanks to Costas Halvresoz for inviting me to visit Austin Willis and for introducing Austin Willis whenever he needed an introduction. Austin recognized in Costas the same gracious host that he had always been and thus could truly be himself for the final performance of his life. Costas also carefully looked over my transcribing and reorganizing of Austin's words for this memoir, and I have great confidence that the Austin Willis we offer readers is not just a poignant, but an authentic telling of his story.

—Ernest J. Dick,
Consulting Archivist,
Historian of Sound and the Moving Image

Index

About the Author

ANGELA MOMBOURQUETTE

Ernest J. Dick lives in Granville Ferry, Nova Scotia. His archival career has focussed on Canada's audio-visual heritage, first at the National Archives of Canada, then at the Canadian Broadcasting Corporation. He has also taught at Saint Mary's University in Halifax and has researched and published works on the history of film and television of Atlantic Canada.